323.43 Val
Valdez, Angela
Gun control /

34028081253933
ATA $35.00 ocn606772281
04/27/12

W9-AJR-632

3 4028 08125 3933
HARRIS COUNTY PUBLIC LIBRARY

Gun Control
Second Edition

POINT
COUNTERPOINT ▷

Gun Control
Second Edition

Angela Valdez & John E. Ferguson Jr.

SERIES EDITOR
Alan Marzilli, M.A., J.D.

CHELSEA HOUSE
An Infobase Learning Company

Gun Control, Second Edition

Copyright © 2012 by Infobase Learning

All rights reserved. No part of this book may be reproduced or utilized in any form or by any means, electronic or mechanical, including photocopying, recording, or by any information storage or retrieval systems, without permission in writing from the publisher. For information, contact:

Chelsea House
An imprint of Infobase Learning
132 West 31st Street
New York, NY 10001

Library of Congress Cataloging-in-Publication Data
Valdez, Angela.
 Gun control / by Angela Valdez and John E. Ferguson Jr.—2nd ed.
 p. cm. — (Point/counterpoint)
 Includes bibliographical references and index.
 ISBN 978-1-60413-905-1 (hardcover)
 1. Gun control—United States—Juvenile literature. 2. Firearms ownership—United States—Juvenile literature. [1. Gun control. 2. Firearms ownership.]
 I. Ferguson, John E. II. Title. III. Series.

 HV7436.V35 2011
 323.4'3—dc22   2011002435

Chelsea House books are available at special discounts when purchased in bulk quantities for businesses, associations, institutions, or sales promotions. Please call our Special Sales Department in New York at (212) 967-8800 or (800) 322-8755.

You can find Chelsea House on the World Wide Web at
http://www.infobaselearning.com.

Text design by Keith Trego
Cover design by Alicia Post
Composition by EJB Publishing Services
Cover printed by Bang Printing, Brainerd, Minn.
Book printed and bound by Bang Printing, Brainerd, Minn.
Date printed: October 2011
Printed in the United States of America

10 9 8 7 6 5 4 3 2 1

This book is printed on acid-free paper.

All links and Web addresses were checked and verified to be correct at the time of publication. Because of the dynamic nature of the Web, some addresses and links may have changed since publication and may no longer be valid.

FOREWORD

Alan Marzilli, M.A., J.D.
Washington, D.C.

The POINT/COUNTERPOINT series offers the reader a greater under-standing of some of the most controversial issues in contemporary American society—issues such as capital punishment, immigration, gay rights, and gun control. We have looked for the most contem-porary issues and have included topics—such as the controversies surrounding "blogging"—that we could not have imagined when the series began.

In each volume, the author has selected an issue of particular importance and set out some of the key arguments on both sides of the issue. Why study both sides of the debate? Maybe you have yet to make up your mind on an issue, and the arguments presented in the book will help you to form an opinion. More likely, however, you will already have an opinion on many of the issues covered by the series. There is always the chance that you will change your opinion after reading the arguments for the other side. But even if you are firmly committed to an issue—for example, school prayer or animal rights—reading both sides of the argument will help you to become a more effective advo-cate for your cause. By gaining an understanding of opposing argu-ments, you can develop answers to those arguments.

Perhaps more importantly, listening to the other side sometimes helps you see your opponent's arguments in a more human way. For example, Sister Helen Prejean, one of the nation's most visible oppo-nents of capital punishment, has been deeply affected by her interac-tions with the families of murder victims. By seeing the families' grief and pain, she understands much better why people support the death penalty, and she is able to carry out her advocacy with a greater sensi-tivity to the needs and beliefs of death penalty supporters.

The books in the series include numerous features that help the reader to gain a greater understanding of the issues. Real-life examples illustrate the human side of the issues. Each chapter also includes excerpts from relevant laws, court cases, and other material, which provide a better foundation for understanding the arguments. The volumes contain citations to relevant sources of law and information, and an appendix guides the reader through the basics of legal research, both on the Internet and in the library. Today, through free Web sites, it is easy to access legal documents, and these books might give you ideas for your own research.

Studying the issues covered by the POINT/COUNTERPOINT series is more than an academic activity. The issues described in the books affect all of us as citizens. They are the issues that today's leaders debate and tomorrow's leaders will decide. While all of the issues covered in the POINT/COUNTERPOINT series are controversial today, and will remain so for the foreseeable future, it is entirely possible that the reader might one day play a central role in resolving the debate. Today it might seem that some debates—such as capital punishment and abortion—will never be resolved.

However, our nation's history is full of debates that seemed as though they never would be resolved, and many of the issues are now well settled—at least on the surface. In the nineteenth century, abolitionists met with widespread resistance to their efforts to end slavery. Ultimately, the controversy threatened the union, leading to the Civil War between the northern and southern states. Today, while a public debate over the merits of slavery would be unthinkable, racism persists in many aspects of society.

Similarly, today nobody questions women's right to vote. Yet at the beginning of the twentieth century, suffragists fought public battles for women's voting rights, and it was not until the passage of the Nineteenth Amendment in 1920 that the legal right of women to vote was established nationwide.

What makes an issue controversial? Often, controversies arise when most people agree that there is a problem but disagree about the best way to solve it. There is little argument that poverty is a major problem in the United States, especially in inner cities and rural areas. Yet, people disagree vehemently about the best way to address the problem. To some, the answer is social programs, such as welfare, food stamps, and public housing. However, many argue that such subsidies encourage dependence on government benefits while unfairly penalizing those who work and pay taxes, and that the real solution is to require people to support themselves.

American society is in a constant state of change, and sometimes modern practices clash with what many consider to be "traditional values," which are often rooted in conservative political views or religious beliefs. Many blame high crime rates, and problems such as poverty, illiteracy, and drug use on the breakdown of the traditional family structure of a married mother and father raising their children. Since the "sexual revolution" of the 1960s and 1970s, sparked in part by the widespread availability of the birth control pill, marriage rates have declined, and the number of children born outside of marriage has increased. The sexual revolution led to controversies over birth control, sex education, and other issues, most prominently abortion. Similarly, the gay rights movement has been challenged as a threat to traditional values. While many gay men and lesbians want to have the same right to marry and raise families as heterosexuals, many politicians and others have challenged gay marriage and adoption as a threat to American society.

Sometimes, new technology raises issues that we have never faced before, and society disagrees about the best solution. Are people free to swap music online, or does this violate the copyright laws that protect songwriters and musicians' ownership of the music that they create? Should scientists use "genetic engineering" to create new crops that are resistant to disease and pests and produce more food, or is it too risky to use a laboratory to create plants that nature never intended? Modern medicine has continued to increase the average lifespan—which is now 77 years, up from under 50 years at the beginning of the twentieth century—but many people are now choosing to die in comfort rather than living with painful ailments in their later years. For doctors, this presents an ethical dilemma: should they allow their patients to die? Should they assist patients in ending their own lives painlessly?

Perhaps the most controversial issues are those that implicate a Constitutional right. The Bill of Rights—the first 10 Amendments to the U.S. Constitution—spells out some of the most fundamental rights that distinguish our democracy from other nations with fewer freedoms. However, the sparsely worded document is open to interpretation, with each side saying that the Constitution is on their side. The Bill of Rights was meant to protect individual liberties; however, the needs of some individuals clash with society's needs. Thus, the Constitution often serves as a battleground between individuals and government officials seeking to protect society in some way. The First Amendment's guarantee of "freedom of speech" leads to some very difficult questions. Some forms of expression—such as burning an American flag—lead to public outrage, but are protected by the First Amendment. Other types of expression that most people find objectionable—such as child pornography—are not protected by the Constitution. The question is not only where to draw the line, but whether drawing lines around constitutional rights threatens our liberty.

The Bill of Rights raises many other questions about individual rights and societal "good." Is a prayer before a high school football game an "establishment of religion" prohibited by the First Amendment? Does the Second Amendment's promise of "the right to bear arms" include concealed handguns? Does stopping and frisking someone standing on a known drug corner constitute "unreasonable search and seizure" in violation of the Fourth Amendment? Although the U.S. Supreme Court has the ultimate authority in interpreting the U.S. Constitution, its answers do not always satisfy the public. When a group of nine people—sometimes by a five-to-four vote—makes a decision that affects hundreds of millions of others, public outcry can be expected. For example, the Supreme Court's 1973 ruling in *Roe v. Wade* that abortion is protected by the Constitution did little to quell the debate over abortion.

Whatever the root of the controversy, the books in the POINT/COUNTERPOINT series seek to explain to the reader the origins of the debate, the current state of the law, and the arguments on either side of the debate. Our hope in creating this series is that readers will be better informed about the issues facing not only our politicians, but all of our nation's citizens, and become more actively involved in resolving these debates, as voters, concerned citizens, journalists, or maybe even elected officials.

Since the first edition of *Gun Control* was published, significant legal changes have affected the landscape of the gun-control debate. For decades, the U.S. Supreme Court had deftly avoided deciding whether the wording of the Second Amendment to the U.S. Constitution granted the right to bear arms as an individual right or to the citizenry collectively in order to form citizen militias. Two decisions challenging handgun bans in Washington, D.C., and Chicago firmly established that owning a gun is a right held by individuals, regardless of their participation or potential participation in militias. However, there remains a great deal of debate regarding the exact scope of that individual right. High-profile shootings by people who had been diagnosed with mental illnesses, along with the relatively ease with which convicted felons may purchase firearms on the black market, raise serious questions about how the sale of firearms could or should be regulated. Interestingly, each high-profile shooting energizes both sides of the gun control lobby, with gun-rights supporters suggesting that if more people were armed, lone gunmen could be stopped more easily before massacring innocent people. With gun control a risky issue for legislators, the volume also examines the court system's role in the debate, specifically whether cities should be allowed to sue gun manufacturers for the costs that gun-related crime impose on communities.

The Politics of Gun Control

In 1968, in the space of about two months, the United States lost two men who had been voices for peace and social change during a decade of tension and turbulent clashes. Civil rights leader Martin Luther King Jr. was shot and killed on April 4, 1968, as he stood on the balcony of the Lorraine Motel in Memphis, Tennessee. James Earl Ray, a career criminal, was convicted of King's murder.

Then, on June 5, 1968, Senator Robert F. Kennedy of New York—a presidential candidate and brother of President John F. Kennedy, who was assassinated on November 22, 1963—was gunned down at the Ambassador Hotel in Los Angeles. Kennedy, 42, had just declared his victory in the Democratic primary in the key state of California. He died a day later. The gunman, Sirhan B. Sirhan, was captured at the scene and later convicted of murder.

These assassinations sparked a national debate over gun violence in the United States, one that has yet to fade from the political landscape. The issue of gun control occupies a singular position in U.S. politics. On this subject, the same liberal advocates who might lobby in the name of free speech for the right to burn the flag or the freedom not to say the Pledge of Allegiance may also oppose the freedom of individuals to own guns. Conservatives who might argue against First Amendment protections for pornography or oppose the rigorous separation of church and state can become staunch defenders of the Bill of Rights when the Second Amendment right to own firearms is discussed prominently alongside freedom of speech and of religion.

The debate is emotionally charged for those on both sides of this issue. Those who believe the government has no authority to regulate firearms summon emotional images of our frontier past, a time when firearms helped earlier Americans form a new country. The icons of U.S. heroism, superiority, and even glamour rely heavily on the symbolic power of the gun: the American Revolutionary soldier, the self-reliant pioneer, the cowboy, the intrepid private detective, and the police officer. The anti-gun-control position is also bolstered by the individualistic tradition in U.S. political philosophy. In this view of politics, each person's rights and values should be protected to the utmost, even if this sometimes supersedes the needs and beliefs of citizens as a group, the government, or the nation.

Those who believe the government has a responsibility to outlaw and restrict firearms are equally adamant about their positions and in their dedication to their views. In recent years, mass shootings and high numbers of inner-city deaths that involved firearms have fueled demands for increasing gun control. Citizens groups have organized protests and campaigns to pressure their representatives in statehouses and on Capitol Hill. For gun-control advocates, the view that gun ownership is a right is an anachronism from a time past when citizens were needed to protect the country from foreign invaders.

In the aftermath of the assassinations of Martin Luther King
Jr. and Robert F. Kennedy, many leading Americans called
for stronger gun control measures. Seen here, famed U.S.
astronaut John Glenn stands in front of the Washington office
of the Emergency Committee for Gun Control in July 1968,
shortly after the King and Kennedy murders.

Elected officials from both major parties have used their opposition to or support for gun control to win elections. According to the Center for Responsive Politics, opponents of gun control contributed, for example, $2.4 million during the 2007–2008 campaign cycle. About 90 percent of the money went to Republican groups and candidates, who are generally strong advocates of gun rights. Gun-control supporters gave almost $58,000 in party and candidate support, with 97 percent of those contributions helping Democrats, who are generally pro-gun control. In addition to promoting candidates who favor their political goals, gun-control and gun-rights groups try to influence legislation in Congress. To this end, advocacy groups spend what they can afford to lobby Congress: Major gun-control groups spent $115,000 on lobbying in 2007–2008. Gun-rights organizations spent almost $3.9 million.[1] The money for these donations comes from a small number of large organizations on either side of the debate. For gun-rights advocates, the National Rifle Association (NRA) has long been their main representative.

THE LETTER OF THE LAW

The Arms Export Control Act (AECA), 22 U.S.C. §2778

The Arms Export Control Act gives the president the authority to control imports and exports of "defense articles," including firearms and ammunition, in furtherance of world peace and the security and foreign policy of the United States. The AECA requires permits and licenses to import and export such articles and prohibits imports from and exports to certain "proscribed countries." The Department of the Treasury administers the import controls of the AECA and has delegated this authority to the Bureau of Alcohol, Tobacco, Firearms, and Explosives. The State Department administers and enforces the AECA's export controls.

The groups supporting gun control are more numerous and include the Brady Center to Prevent Gun Violence and the Violence Policy Center (VPC).[2]

Current Regulations on Firearms

The Second Amendment of the U.S. Constitution, in its entirety, states: "A well-regulated Militia, being necessary to the security of a free State, the right of the people to keep and bear Arms, shall not be infringed." The interpretation of this simple statement had led to contentious debates in the centuries since the amendment was adopted in 1791.

The first Supreme Court case to consider federal regulation of firearms in light of the Second Amendment was the case of *United States v. Miller*.[3] Jack Miller was a member of the Irish O'Malley gang and had participated in several bank robberies. When four men against whom he had testified broke out of prison, Miller began to fear for his life. Historians have speculated that this fear drove Miller to keep a weapon by his side during all his travels. On April 18, 1938, Miller and Frank Layton drove from Oklahoma to Arkansas and were charged with unlawfully transporting a firearm—in this case, an unregistered sawed-off shotgun—over state lines without a permit, in violation of the National Firearms Act of 1934. After their arrest and indictment, they were charged with violating the act, which prohibited the unlicensed transportation of short-barreled guns. In their defense, Miller and Layton pleaded that the law violated the Second Amendment. The government appealed a district court ruling that had been granted in the defendants' favor.

In a ruling issued in 1939, the Supreme Court held that the "obvious purpose" of the Second Amendment was "to assure the continuation and render possible the effectiveness" of state militias. The Court added, "It must be interpreted and applied with that end in view."[4] (The ruling overturned the previous ruling and upheld charges against Miller and Layton.)

Gun-control supporters believe the Second Amendment requires a connection to military service for the bearing of arms to be protected. Gun-rights advocates, however, believe the opposite:

FROM THE BENCH

United States v. Miller, 307 U.S. 174 (1939)

In the absence of any evidence tending to show that possession or use of a "shotgun having a barrel of less than eighteen inches [45.7 centimeters] in length" at this time has some reasonable relationship to the preservation or efficiency of a well regulated militia, we cannot say that the Second Amendment guarantees the right to keep and bear such an instrument. Certainly it is not within judicial notice that this weapon is any part of the ordinary military equipment or that its use could contribute to the common defense. . . .

The Constitution as originally adopted granted to the Congress power "To provide for calling forth the Militia to execute the Laws of the Union, suppress Insurrections and repel Invasions; To provide for organizing, arming, and disciplining, the Militia, and for governing such Part of them as may be employed in the Service of the United States, reserving to the States respectively, the Appointment of the Officers, and the Authority of training the Militia according to the discipline prescribed by Congress." With obvious purpose to assure the continuation and render possible the effectiveness of such forces the declaration and guarantee of the Second Amendment were made. It must be interpreted and applied with that end in view.

The Militia which the States were expected to maintain and train is set in contrast with Troops which they were forbidden to keep without the consent of Congress. The sentiment of the time strongly disfavored standing armies; the common view was that adequate defense of country and laws could be secured through the Militia—civilians primarily, soldiers on occasion.

The signification attributed to the term Militia appears from the debates in the Convention, the history and legislation of Colonies and States, and the writings of approved commentators. These show plainly enough that the Militia comprised all males physically capable of acting in concert for the common defense. "A body of citizens enrolled for military discipline." And further, that ordinarily when called for service these men were expected to appear bearing arms supplied by themselves and of the kind in common use at the time.

that a connection to military service must be disproved before the right to bear arms can be limited. Pointing to historical evidence that Revolutionary War–era militias required their members to bring their own arms, they argue that the Second Amendment was meant to make it possible for citizens to buy and keep their own weapons. In their narrow interpretation of the *Miller* ruling, gun-control opponents believe the Court approved the restriction of the right to bear arms *only* if the weapon had no connection to military or militia use—a hard case to make if, as they believe, almost every gun could be used for militia service.

In response to rulings such as *Miller* and pressure from both sides of the debate, state and federal gun-control laws attempt to reduce violence by barring civilians from owning certain high-risk military weapons (machine guns and some semiautomatic assault weapons), and by prohibiting certain groups (felons, children, and people with diminished mental capacity) from owning guns. Federal laws such as the Gun Control Act of 1968 require manufacturers to imprint each firearm with a serial number, while the Brady Handgun Violence Prevention Act of 1993 requires background checks on licensed sales of firearms.

For decades, a debate raged as to whether the Second Amendment applied to state governments as well as to the federal government. The 2010 Supreme Court decision *McDonald v. Chicago* settled much of this debate by clarifying that the Second Amendment applies to all levels of government.[5] The Court also reaffirmed *District of Columbia v. Heller*, a 2008 decision that found that the Second Amendment applies to the individual and protects gun ownership for purposes of self-protection.[6] While these decisions have modified the gun-control controversy, they have not solved all points of disagreement.

Where the Debate Stands

Advocates of gun control believe that many lives will be saved if the government makes it even harder for people to own firearms. They advocate waiting periods on gun purchases and limits on the number of guns one person can buy in a month. They present statistics that compare high numbers of gun-related deaths in the United States with lower numbers in countries with more stringent regulations on gun ownership and usage. The most absolute gun-control advocates believe the Supreme Court misinterpreted the Second Amendment, and that it should grant the right to bear arms *only* in the context of military service.

More moderate gun-control advocates believe that the *McDonald* and *Heller* rulings should be interpreted narrowly, protecting restrictions on categories of weapons (such as military-style weapons and semiautomatic pistols), on ownership by felons or people with diminished capacities, and on places in which guns may be carried (such as schools, places of worship, and places where alcohol is served.)

Gun-control advocates also point to much-publicized tragedies such as gun-related domestic violence and public shootings, including at schools and workplaces, as reason for their desire to regulate and/or restrict gun ownership. One such example was the case of a series of sniper attacks in the Washington, D.C., area. In the fall of 2002, the area around Washington was traumatized by a series of murders committed using a sniper rifle. After three weeks of frightening uncertainty, with 10 people dead and three wounded, police arrested John Allen Muhammad and Lee Boyd Malvo. These two soon faced multiple murder charges in which some of the strongest evidence against them came from the "ballistic fingerprint" of a gun allegedly found in their car.[7]

The case increased public interest in creating a national electronic database of "ballistic fingerprints" based on test-firing records that gun manufacturers would be required to create for each gun before sale. The U.S. Bureau of Alcohol, Tobacco, Firearms and Explosives (ATF) already helps police investigators with its Integrated Ballistic Identification System (IBIS), which makes automated comparisons that can sometimes find important links between crimes. An ATF report said, "Numerous violent crimes involving firearms have been solved through use of the system, many of which would not have been solved without it."[8]

Gun-rights advocates, such as the NRA, oppose ideas such as ballistic fingerprinting, arguing that these measures are ineffective, cost prohibitive, and ultimately only punish law-abiding citizens. In a position paper, the NRA argues that the state of Maryland, which adopted a ballistic-fingerprinting law in 2000, had significantly reduced the sale of handguns, and had spent some $3 million in doing so, but had not solved any crimes using its database. It further argued that a gun's "fingerprint" changes with age and use and that criminals can alter the print further by changing a gun's parts.[9]

Approximately one-third of U.S. households contain at least one firearm; these guns are most often purchased for sport, hunting, or self-defense.[10] Until the past few years, it was possible to debate whether the Second Amendment protected the individual right to own firearms. Recent U.S. Supreme Court decisions, however, have held that it does. Opponents of gun control believe that it limits law-abiding citizens' access to guns that are valuable for self-defense and recreation. They argue that because only law-abiding citizens will obey gun laws, such laws will give the advantage to criminals. They believe that the Second Amendment guarantees an individual right to bear arms, almost unconditionally.

Summary

Despite all the constitutional arguments on both sides, the debate over the control of guns can be seen as cultural—a rift between those who have been raised in a culture in which the tradition of gun ownership is personally meaningful, and those who have not and are uncomfortable around firearms. To say this, of course, is to oversimplify the argument; sub-arguments abound concerning, for example, self-defense, government interference in personal liberties, the balance of power between citizens and criminals, and the risk inherent in the very presence of a gun. Whatever the motivations, though, the public debate is based on law and policy—on interpretation of the Second Amendment, on the relationship of gun incidence to crime rates, and on the risk of gun-related injury to the public.

Gun Activists Misconstrue the Second Amendment

The NRA and anti-gun-control groups use the Second Amendment to anchor their position that gun ownership in the United States should be unrestricted or only minimally restricted. Critics say these activists latch on to the superficial meaning of the Second Amendment without acknowledging the limits on gun ownership set forward by the very people who drafted the Constitution. A former Supreme Court chief justice, Warren Burger, voiced this position powerfully in 1991:

> [The Second Amendment] is the subject of one of the greatest pieces of fraud, I repeat the word *fraud*, on the American public by special interest groups that I have ever seen in my lifetime. . . . [Opponents of gun control have] misled the American people and they, I regret to say, they have had far too much influence on the

Congress of the United States than as a citizen I would like to see—and I am a gun man.[1]

In Burger's view, the Second Amendment cannot be viewed as permitting citizens to own arms without restriction, and to argue otherwise is to misrepresent the Second Amendment's language.

The "right to bear arms" depends on the need for a militia.

Gun-control advocates had long argued that the Second Amendment, unlike other amendments, cannot be separated from its stated purpose, the need for a militia. The First Amendment specifically enumerates the rights of speech, religion, and the press: "Congress shall make no law respecting an establishment of religion, or prohibiting the free exercise thereof; or abridging the freedom of speech, or of the press." These rights are plainly stated, with no exceptions specified.

The Second Amendment, however, begins with a preamble that states the purpose for the right: "a well-regulated militia." By stating that purpose first, gun-control advocates believe, the framers of the Constitution intended to set boundaries on the right. They interpret the preamble's "A well regulated Militia, being necessary to the security of a free State" to mean "For the sole reason that a militia is needed to protect a free nation."

James Madison, who penned the Second Amendment, made the defense-related goal of his law apparent in his original draft: "The right of the people to keep and bear arms shall not be infringed; a well armed and well regulated militia being the best security of a free country; but no person religiously scrupulous of bearing arms shall be compelled to render military service in person." The last clause addressed those with religious objections to military service and exempted them from duty. Although the Senate ultimately dropped the religious exemption, Madison's use of it establishes his understanding that to "bear Arms" was to provide military service, not to simply own guns. While the U.S. Supreme Court later rejected this interpretation of the Second Amendment, gun-control activists continue to press for laws that limit gun ownership, rejecting the concept that widespread gun ownership is needed to maintain order.

As there is no longer a need for a militia, there is no longer a need to bear arms.

In the late twentieth century, self-organized groups of citizens calling themselves militias began cropping up in rural and suburban communities. These loosely organized groups have little in common with a "well-regulated Militia." Unlike today's "citizen militias," composed of antigovernment extremists, the militias of the early United States were by definition compulsory and dedicated to protecting the nation. At the time of the signing of the Constitution in 1787, virtually all able-bodied white men in the fledgling states were required to report for service in state militias. These state-run forces performed the duties of a standing army in a country that was fearful of concentrating too much power with the central government.

In 1903, the National Guard was created. Designed to meet many of the same needs as the early militia, as well as many new roles, the National Guard became the institution that performs military and paramilitary needs in the United States when needed, and then the participants go back to their daily lives when the crisis passes. Gun-control advocates point out that the National Guard effectively eliminates the need for a militia. Without a militia, the need for people to arm themselves privately also is eliminated, as the National Guard provides weapons for service members when they are needed, and securely stores them when inactive.[2]

"The right to bear arms" is not an absolute right.

The freedoms set forth in the Bill of Rights, gun-control advocates argue, have never been absolute—that is, there are exceptions to them. As Justice Oliver Wendell Holmes famously declared in *Schenck v. United States* (1919), the freedom of speech does not protect people who mischievously yell "fire" in a crowded theater—for the government has an interest in protecting its citizens and so must weigh the public interest against that individual right.[3] Nor does the freedom of speech protect newspapers that knowingly publish false information. Likewise, for most moderate policy makers, the debate is not about *whether* the Constitution allows for gun control; it is about the *extent* to which the state and federal governments should regulate ownership and use. Most U.S. citizens seem to favor some kind of gun control. A poll conducted in April 2010 by CBS News and the *New York Times* found that 82 percent of those polled think gun-control laws should be either made stricter or kept as they are, with only 16 percent favoring making gun-control laws less strict.[4]

Centrist groups, such as the Brady Center to Prevent Gun Violence (named in honor of presidential aide James Brady who was wounded during an assassination attempt on President Ronald Reagan in 1981) believe that hunters and those who use firearms for legitimate sport should be allowed to continue their hobbies. Hunting is a true pastime in the United States and contributes to the happiness of millions of citizens. The careful regulation or outright banning of handguns and assault weapons would, the Brady organization and others argue, keep guns designed to kill *people* out of circulation, allowing hunters to preserve their pastime.[5]

Others take a more radical approach. Some gun-control advocates say the Second Amendment has become an anachronism, a relic that is no longer applicable in modern life. Semiautomatic handguns and assault rifles, which did not exist during the American Revolution, have caused problems that the authors of the Constitution could never have envisioned. These gun-control advocates lobby for an outright ban of all guns. Still other gun-control advocates claim they are countering the extremism of staunch gun-rights activists. These extreme gun-rights activists argue that the Second Amendment provides an incontrovertible privilege to own guns to all U.S. citizens, even those who may pose a threat to others, such as criminals and those with diminished capacities. Often, the NRA argues that this right is based on the possibility of tyranny. If our government became undemocratic and repressive, they argue, citizens would need to protect themselves.

Gun-control advocates say this logic leads straight to a dangerous result: citizens armed with ever-more-dangerous weapons such as rocket launchers, missiles, and even nuclear arms. If one accepts that the Second Amendment provides a blanket protection of the right to bear arms, of any type, by anyone, and if this right is aimed at allowing citizens to rise up against their own government, then it follows that ordinary people should have easy access to military weapons. U.S. citizens would need bazookas and tanks, grenade launchers, and nuclear weapons to fight the full force of the country's military. In addition to the obvious impracticality of this situation, gun-control advocates say, the Constitution actually prohibits citizens from going to war against their government. The crime of treason is spelled out in Article III, Section 3: "Treason against the United States shall consist only in levying war against them, or in adhering to their enemies, giving them aid and comfort." Gun-control advocates say that an unlimited right to bear arms would be tantamount to including a suicide clause in the Constitution.

The Supreme Court allows for some arms restriction.

Gun-rights supporters have applauded recent Supreme Court decisions overruling several decades of lower-court rulings that rejected the idea of gun ownership being an individual right. Yet even these decisions confirm that gun ownership is not an absolute right. As Justice Antonin Scalia explains in his concurrence to the *McDonald* decision, "No fundamental right—not even the First Amendment—is absolute."[6]

The legislative aftermath is even clearer on this issue. Following the *Heller* decision in 2008, Washington, D.C., complied with the Supreme Court's decision by allowing guns in the city, but established extensive bureaucratic registration hurdles. These included waiting periods, limitations on bullet capacity, limitations on

FROM THE BENCH

District of Columbia v. Heller, 554 U.S. 570 (2008)

Like most rights, the right secured by the Second Amendment is not unlimited. From Blackstone through the 19th-century cases, commentators and courts routinely explained that the right was not a right to keep and carry any weapon whatsoever in any manner whatsoever and for whatever purpose. For example, the majority of the 19th-century courts to consider the question held that prohibitions on carrying concealed weapons were lawful under the Second Amendment or state analogues. Although we do not undertake an exhaustive historical analysis today of the full scope of the Second Amendment, nothing in our opinion should be taken to cast doubt on longstanding prohibitions on the possession of firearms by felons and the mentally ill, or laws forbidding the carrying of firearms in sensitive places such as schools and government buildings, or laws imposing conditions and qualifications on the commercial sale of arms.

McDonald v. Chicago, 561 U.S. ___, 130 S.Ct. 3020 (2010)

It is important to keep in mind that *Heller*, while striking down a law that prohibited the possession of handguns in the home, recognized that the right to keep and bear arms is not "a right to keep and carry any weapon whatsoever in any manner whatsoever and for whatever purpose." We made it clear in *Heller* that our holding did not cast doubt on such longstanding regulatory measures as "prohibitions on the possession of firearms by felons and the mentally ill," "laws forbidding the carrying Opinion of the Court of firearms in sensitive places such as schools and government buildings, or laws imposing conditions and qualifications on the commercial sale of arms." We repeat those assurances here. Despite municipal respondents' doomsday proclamations, incorporation does not imperil every law regulating firearms.

types of guns, required classes, time at a firing range (even though there were no public firing ranges available), instruction by a police-certified trainer, and even future requirements of micro-stamping identification that had yet to be implemented by gun manufacturers. For many residents, this process could take several weeks. If a person failed to renew their license on the gun every three years, the gun could be confiscated and the owner could be fined $1,000. These requirements are being challenged in court, but lower-court decisions seem to indicate that at least some of these requirements will pass constitutional muster. Although many have requested registration information after the *Heller* decision was passed, the regulations have kept actual registration at a lower level than anticipated by lawmakers.[7]

The *McDonald* decision also gives support for gun-control advocates. Justice Samuel Alito seeks to assuage the concerns of those supporting gun regulations by explaining that while the Second Amendment *does* protect an individuals right to own a gun, it *does not* mean that gun ownership cannot be restricted. He explains:

> It is important to keep in mind that *Heller*, while strik-ing down a law that prohibited the possession of hand-guns in the home, recognized that the right to keep and bear arms is not "a right to keep and carry any weapon whatsoever in any manner whatsoever and for whatever purpose." We made it clear in *Heller* that our holding did not cast doubt on such longstanding regulatory measures as "prohibitions on the possession of firearms by felons and the mentally ill," "laws forbidding the carrying of firearms in sensitive places such as schools and government buildings, or laws imposing conditions and qualifications on the commercial sale of arms." We repeat those assurances here. Despite municipal respondents' doomsday proclamations, incorporation does not imperil every law regulating firearms.[8]

Former Chief Justice Burger said:

> The very language of the Second Amendment refutes any argument that it was intended to guarantee every citizen an unfettered right to any kind of weapon. . . . [S]urely the Second Amendment does not remotely guarantee every person the constitutional right to have a "Saturday Night Special" or a machine gun without any regulation whatever. There is no support in the Constitution for the argument that federal and state governments are powerless to regulate the purchase of such firearms.[9]

The American "gun heritage" is largely mythical.

Gun-control opponents often sell their case by relying on the symbolic power of the history of gun use in the United States. Historians and gun-control advocates, however, have called the image of the gun-toting colonist into question. Michael Bellesiles, a history professor at Emory University, published findings in 1999 that suggested that few U.S. citizens owned guns in the nation's early years. According to his survey of estate wills, fewer than 10 percent of citizens owned firearms until 1850.[10] Today, more than 35 percent of U.S. households contain guns.[11] Hollywood Westerns often portrayed frontier towns as wild outposts where the marshal or sheriff was no match for sharpshooting bandits. Most western towns, however, had strict laws restricting gun ownership within city limits. Samuel Colt, the gun manufacturer credited with encouraging the image of the gun-slinging American man, also coined a slogan that encompasses the mythological passion of the nation's love affair with the gun: "God may have made men, but Sam Colt made them equal." It says something about the true role of guns in U.S. history that Colt's brother John was tried in 1841 for murdering a creditor—with a hammer.[12]

Bellesiles's conclusions became the subject of an extensive lobbying campaign by gun advocates, including the NRA and columnists in conservative journals. He received death threats, and his supporters and employers received angry letters. On a more scholarly level, some academics challenged the accuracy of his reports on early American probate records and questioned whether public records really would have existed for *all* the guns actually available to early Americans. Along with specific answers to critics, Bellesiles has stated that a flood at his office destroyed important research notes for his book. The book won the prestigious Bancroft Prize, and Bellesiles received statements of support from the American Historical Association and other reputable scholarly organizations. On the other hand, Emory University took the critics' charges of sloppiness and even falsification seriously enough to investigate. The Emory investigating committee's report supported several of the charges. In October 2002, Bellesiles resigned his professorship, citing a "hostile environment."[13]

Summary

The most adamant supporters of gun control argue that the Second Amendment refers to the use of weapons for national defense and does not confer an individual right to bear arms. Some centrist gun-control advocates want to preserve hunting and sport uses of guns and point to Supreme Court decisions that confirm gun ownership is not an absolute right. Gun-control advocates generally see the pro-gun rhetoric about physically fighting a tyrannical government as both impractical and alarming, and they note that it essentially legitimizes the crime of treason. There is also the question of whether guns were as important in the days of the Founding Fathers as gun advocates would have us believe.

The Second Amendment Remains Relevant

Early American colonists had many uses for firearms. A good musket could supply a family with food, protect against attacks by wild animals, and serve as a weapon against the indigenous Indian populations who objected, often violently, to the colonial presence. After years of oppressive British rule, the colonists found a new use for firearms: revolution. The original 13 colonies, with their growing economic and cultural development, had become dissatisfied with what they saw as foreign rule. King George III of Great Britain, unlike the increasingly rebellious colonists, believed his nation was the motherland and the distant American colonies were her unruly children. The colonists bristled under the king's relentless demands. They were taxed but did not receive representation in the British government. They were forced to give lodging to British troops and to provide a market for British goods. In

1776, the colonies declared independence and went to war with Great Britain.

The American Revolution, which ended in 1783, would not have been possible without firearms. Historians believe the superior range of the "Pennsylvania rifle," a product designed and manufactured by German settlers, was responsible for giving the revolutionists an early advantage in battles against British troops. Time after time, the people who support the right to bear arms return to the early American stories of oppression, rebellion, and eventual freedom. The American Revolution sets the backdrop for the argument for the right to bear arms.

The current gun-control debate, however, really begins with the Second Amendment to the Constitution. The U.S. Constitution created the framework for the nation's legal system, the foundation upon which the structure of American society is built. The men who wrote the Constitution engaged in a long debate over the 27 words of the Second Amendment: "A well-regulated Militia, being necessary to the security of a free State, the right of the people to keep and bear Arms, shall not be infringed."

When the Framers drafted the Constitution, military defense was a necessary consideration. The substance of their debate is of great concern to modern policy makers, as both advocates and opponents of gun control make historical arguments about the meaning of the Second Amendment. Each side uses differences in interpretation to find evidence that the Framers intended to draft an amendment that supports one side over the other.

Seen from the historical perspective advocated by gun-rights supporters, there were two main motivations for the Second Amendment. First, U.S. citizens had inherited from the British system a respect for the rights of citizens to arm themselves. The judge-made English "common law" included a provision protecting the right to bear arms. In a sense, this argument asserts that the right to bear arms was passed down, along with other traditions, from the British motherland to the American colonies. Second, the revolutionary experience had instilled in the colonists a fundamental distrust of centralized governments. A permanent national military, or standing army, epitomized the kind of centralized power that concerned them. A system of state militias was seen as a preventive measure against dependency on a standing army. In each state, militias of self-armed men were called upon to defend their country themselves. By relying on loosely organized groups of armed citizens, the authors of the Constitution believed they could protect the young nation from arbitrary and tyrannical rule.

Gun-control opponents quote the Framers themselves in defending their interpretation of history. Patrick Henry said at Virginia's ratification convention, "The great object is that every man be armed. Every man who is able may have a gun." Samuel Adams remarked at the Massachusetts convention: "The Constitution shall never be construed to prevent the people of the United States who are peaceable citizens from keeping their own arms." John Adams noted: "Arms in the hands of citizens may be used at individual discretion, in private self-defense."[1] Thomas Jefferson modeled much of his thought on the work of the Italian philosopher/criminologist Cesare Beccaria, who argued the absurdity of restricting arms in order to prevent crime:

> The laws that forbid the carrying of arms ... disarm those only who are neither inclined nor determined to commit crimes. Can it be supposed that those who have the courage to violate the most sacred laws of humanity, the most important of the code, will respect the less important and arbitrary ones, which can be violated with impunity, and which, if strictly obeyed, would put an end to personal liberty—so dear to men, so dear to the enlightened legislator—and subject innocent persons to all the vexations that the guilty alone ought to suffer? Such laws make things worse for the assaulted and bet-

ter for the assailants; they serve rather to encourage than prevent homicides, for an unarmed man may be attacked with greater confidence than an armed man.[2]

Jefferson copied this passage in its entirety into his personal "commonplace book." *The Federalist Papers*—two volumes of essays printed in 1787 and 1788 that argued in favor of ratifying the Constitution—also contain arguments in favor of arming the citizenry. James Madison, the author of the Second Amendment, noted in *The Federalist Papers* that U.S. citizens had "the advantage of being armed"—an advantage lost in other nations, where governments did not trust armed citizens.[3] Alexander Hamilton wrote:

> [I]f circumstances should at any time oblige the government to form an army of any magnitude, that army can never be formidable to the liberties of the people while there is a large body of citizens, little if at all inferior to them in discipline and the use of arms, who stand ready to defend their rights and those of their fellow citizens.[4]

Another saying of Hamilton's is quoted even more often: "The best we can hope for concerning the people at large is that they be properly armed."[5]

When gun-control advocates argue that the modern National Guard fulfills the duties of the militia of the Second Amendment, opponents counter that the militias intended by the Framers were grassroots citizens organizations. All eligible men were de facto members. The National Guard, a system of armed forces run by each of the 50 states established in 1903, is too formal, in the view of gun-control opponents, to replace the citizen-run militias. In 1920, Congress deemed the National Guard to be only one part, not the whole, of the "Militia of the United States."

Militias were frequently deployed for community and national defense. They were called upon to quell uprisings and rebellions—among slaves, native populations, or whites—as well as to defend the nation during the War of 1812 and the Civil War (1861–1865). One year after the addition of the Second Amendment, Congress passed the Militia Act of 1792, which required all able-bodied free white men to arm themselves and serve as members of local militias. It appears clear to gun-rights advocates that the militia applied to almost everyone, at least as far as most laws at the time did. Akhil Reed Amar of Yale Law School and Alan Hirsch, a former *Yale Law Journal* editor, wrote:

> We recall that the Framers' militia was not an elite fighting force but the entire citizenry of the time: all able-bodied adult white males. Since the Second Amendment explicitly declares that its purpose is to preserve a well-regulated militia, the right to bear arms was universal in scope. The vision animating the amendment was nothing less than popular sovereignty—applied in the military realm. The Framers recognized that self-government requires the People's access to bullets as well as ballots. The armed citizenry (militia) was expected to protect against not only foreign enemies, but also a potentially tyrannical federal government. In short, the right to bear arms was intended to ensure that our government remained in the hands of the People.[6]

The right to bear arms applies to individuals.

The Second Amendment is contained in the Bill of Rights, the first 10 amendments to the Constitution. Gun-control opponents believe that the Bill of Rights as a whole was meant to protect *individual* liberties. To bolster the historical basis of their position, gun-control opponents return to the words of the Framers: Madison wrote that the Bill of Rights was "calculated to secure the personal rights of the people." Albert Gallatin, treasury secretary under Thomas Jefferson, said, "[I]t establishes some rights of the individual as unalienable and which consequently, no majority has a right to deprive them of." [7]

In the Declaration of Independence, the document that announced the colonists' intention to break from British rule, Jefferson wrote that "all men are created equal" and "are endowed by their Creator with certain unalienable rights"—that is, rights that cannot be taken away from them by any government. In contrast with the natural rights of the people, he wrote that government derives its powers from the consent of the governed. Gun-control opponents rely on an interpretation of the Constitution in which the term "the people" applies to each individual person in the United States, irrespective of that person's membership in a larger organization, such as a militia or a church.

Understanding the idea of a militia as a loose group of individual citizens, and not a formal, government-sponsored military body, is a key to understanding the scope of the debate over the Second Amendment. Gun-control opponents believe that the Framers intended the Second Amendment to be interpreted as a right granted to each person as a self-sufficient entity. This position draws on the legacy of individual rights in the United States, on the belief that human rights, by definition, belong to the people as individuals, not as a group. Other individual rights

THE LETTER OF THE LAW

The National Firearms Act of 1934

The National Firearms Act regulates certain classes of firearms, such as machine guns, short-barrel rifles, short-barrel shotguns, silencers, and destructive devices. The NFA requires that these weapons be registered by their makers, manufacturers, and importers and imposes taxes on transactions involving such weapons.

protected by the Constitution include the freedom of speech, the freedom of religion, and the right to be protected from unreasonable searches and seizures.

An interpretation of the rights of the people as the rights of individuals was offered in the case of *United States v. Verdugo-Urquidez* (1990):

> "[T]he people" seems to have been a term of art employed in select parts of the Constitution. The Preamble declares that the Constitution is ordained and established by "the People of the United States." The Second Amendment protects "the right of the people to keep and bear Arms," and the Ninth and Tenth Amendments provide that certain rights and powers are retained by and reserved to "the people." . . . It suggests that "the people" protected by the Fourth Amendment, and by the First and Second Amendments, and to whom rights and powers are reserved in the Ninth and Tenth Amendments, refers to a class of persons who are a part of a national community or who have otherwise developed sufficient connection with this country to be considered part of that community.[8]

The Supreme Court supports an individual-rights interpretation.

In 2008, the Supreme Court case of *District of Columbia v. Heller* finally answered some of the most contentious questions involving gun control. Acting on behalf of citizens in the District of Columbia, several groups supported the case to test the city's outright ban on handguns. Since the District is under federal control, this was simply a case of whether the Second Amendment protected an individual's right to gun ownership or whether the amendment protects the right of state militias to be armed. The Court found that the right to bear arms is an individual right and that the federal government cannot infringe on the right of a person to own a gun for the purpose of self-defense. While this decision was viewed as a victory for gun-rights proponents, the ruling was limited in that it applied only to the federal government, with no clear indication as to whether the Second Amendment's protections were extended to state and local governments.[9]

Two years later, in 2010, the Supreme Court answered that question as well in the case of *McDonald v. Chicago.* The case involved Chicago's 28-year-old ban on handguns, as well as similar gun restriction in Oak Park, Illinois. Mayor Richard M. Daley of Chicago argued that his city's gun laws, the most restrictive in the nation, were necessary to protect citizens from gun violence. He also argued that the ban did not violate the Second Amendment because the amendment only applied to the federal government, not to states or cities such as Chicago. The plaintiffs, four Chicago residents and the NRA, argued that the *Heller* decision made clear that the right to bear arms was an individual right to protect oneself and, like the other individual rights in the Bill of Rights, it must apply to states and cities as well.

Writing for the majority in the 5-4 decision, Justice Samuel Alito explained:

> In *Heller,* we held that the Second Amendment protects the right to possess a handgun in the home for the purpose of self-defense. Unless considerations of *stare decisis* counsel otherwise, a provision of the Bill of Rights that protects a right that is fundamental from an American perspective applies equally to the Federal Government and the States.[10]

The right to bear arms is fundamental to liberty.
Gun-control opponents view the right to bear arms as an individual liberty and feel that efforts to limit access to guns are tantamount to repression. Furthermore, they believe the

FROM THE BENCH

District of Columbia v. Heller, 554 U.S. 570 (2008)

We turn finally to the law at issue here. As we have said, the law totally bans handgun possession in the home. It also requires that any lawful firearm in the home be disassembled or bound by a trigger lock at all times, rendering it inoperable.

As the quotations earlier in this opinion demonstrate, the inherent right of self-defense has been central to the Second Amendment right. The handgun ban amounts to a prohibition of an entire class of "arms" that is overwhelmingly chosen by American society for that lawful purpose. The prohibition extends, moreover, to the home, where the need for defense of self, family, and property is most acute. Under any of the standards of scrutiny that we have applied to enumerated constitutional rights, banning from the home "the most preferred firearm in the nation to 'keep' and use for protection of one's home and family," would fail constitutional muster. . . .

In sum, we hold that the District's ban on handgun possession in the home violates the Second Amendment, as does its prohibition against rendering any lawful firearm in the home operable for the purpose of immediate self-defense. Assuming that Heller is not disqualified from the exercise of Second Amendment rights, the District must permit him to register his handgun and must issue him a license to carry it in the home.

McDonald v. Chicago, 561 U.S. ___, 130 S.Ct. 3020 (2010)

In *Heller*, however, we expressly rejected the argument that the scope of the Second Amendment right should be determined by judicial interest balancing, and this Court decades ago abandoned "the notion that the Fourteenth Amendment applies to the States only a watered-down, subjective version of the individual guarantees of the Bill of Rights." . . .

In *Heller*, we held that the Second Amendment protects the right to possess a handgun in the home for the purpose of self-defense. Unless considerations of *stare decisis* counsel otherwise, a provision of the Bill of Rights that protects a right that is fundamental from an American perspective applies equally to the Federal Government and the States. We therefore hold that the Due Process Clause of the Fourteenth Amendment incorporates the Second Amendment right recognized in *Heller*.

liberties that made the United States into the strong nation that it is today encompass the right to bear arms. Charlton Heston, the actor who was best known for his roles in such films as *The Ten Commandments* (1956), *Ben-Hur* (1959), and *Planet of the Apes* (1968), became president of the NRA in 1998 and spoke at Harvard Law School in 1999 about his passionate view on gun control:

> I believe that we are again engaged in a great civil war, a cultural war that's about to hijack your birthright to think and say what resides in your heart. I fear you no longer trust the pulsing lifeblood of liberty inside you . . . the stuff that made this country rise from wilderness into the miracle that it is.[11]

The Second Amendment is permanently connected to colonial times and the nation's efforts to free itself from foreign rule. These links to great struggles imbue the right to bear arms with feelings of power and strength, qualities that are part of the American psyche. Neal Knox, a libertarian member of the NRA who helped to guide the organization in the 1970s, has said that "gun control is about power; the person with the guns has the power."[12]

Gun-rights activists see the right to bear arms as emblematic of a larger conservative effort to keep the government out of private lives. The less control the government has over individual behavior, conservatives believe, the better. Although opponents of gun control tend to be politically on the right, some extreme leftists—notably the African-American separatist Black Panther Party—have also advocated using guns in self-defense against the government in times of repression. Finally, most gun advocates contend that their position is in fact a more traditional interpretation of the Second Amendment, which argues that the Framers of the Constitution wanted to ensure that U.S. citizens had the ability to overthrow tyrannical or oppressive rulers.

Summary

The right to keep and bear arms is a guarantee of American freedom. The prevalent pro-gun view associates individual firearm ownership with the memory that, at the time of the Constitution's framing, the newly independent citizens rejected a professional standing army in favor of an informal citizens militia. The Supreme Court in the *Heller* and *McDonald* decisions found that gun ownership is an individual right and that the Second Amendment protects that right against infringement from either federal or state governments. Although there are some left-wing gun supporters, most pro-gun advocacy is closely associated with a conservative individualism that also opposes government interference in people's personal lives.

Gun-Control Laws Reduce Violence

The gun-related death rate in the United States is higher than that of any other industrialized nation. Almost 30,000 people in the country die every year from gunshot wounds.[1] Young people are especially at risk: In 1998, for example, an average of 10 children and teenagers were killed every day by firearms, and firearms were the second most frequent cause of death *overall* for U.S. citizens ages 15 to 24.[2] Gun-control advocates predict that gunfire may soon surpass cars as the leading cause of unnatural death among children. Researchers Franklin Zimring and Gordon Hawkins cite the use of firearms in assault and robbery as "the single environmental feature of American society that is most clearly linked to the extraordinary death rate from interpersonal violence in the United States." These researchers conclude that, "without strategies for the reduction of firearm

41

use in assaults, no policy can be accurately characterized as directed at the reduction of American lethal violence."[3]

The high rates of gun-related death in the U.S. are a result of permissive gun laws.

Permissive U.S. gun laws generally make it easy for adults to purchase firearms. Existing restrictions ban certain groups from purchasing guns—children, people with diminished mental capacity, and criminals—and require background checks and waiting periods on licensed sales. Yet many sales still proceed with no background check on the buyer, and few records of who buys guns are kept.

One basic truth leads the argument for gun control: Guns are deadlier than any other weapon. An assault with a firearm is five times more likely to lead to death than is an assault involving a knife. Furthermore, about 40 percent of U.S. households own firearms. Because of this combination of lethality and prevalence, guns are used in most murders in the United States. In 2007, guns were involved in the top two most common violence-related deaths in the United States (suicide with a firearm was No. 1; homicide with a firearm was No. 2).[4]

Historically, the United States has had the highest rates of murder and other violent crime among all the industrialized nations. The United States is, among industrialized democracies, the only nation in which firearms are the cause of the majority of homicides. How do we know this? The government has collected statistics on homicide and other violent crimes in the United States since the early twentieth century. Historians believe the U.S. murder rate first peaked in 1933 at about 10 murders per every 100,000 citizens per year. The following years marked the beginning of a steady decline in the murder rate, which fell until the mid-1940s, rose slightly at the end of World War II, and continued to decline until 1958, when the rate hit 4.5 murders per 100,000 citizens. In the mid-1960s, the homicides increased rapidly, hitting rates of 9 per 100,000, and did not plateau until the late 1970s. After falling in the early 1980s, the

Americans divided on gun control

Half of Americans think state and local governments should be able to pass gun control laws.

A closer look
Percent who favor gun control

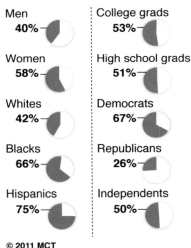

Men
40%

College grads
53%

Women
58%

High school grads
51%

Whites
42%

Democrats
67%

Blacks
66%

Republicans
26%

Hispanics
75%

Independents
50%

© 2011 **MCT**
Source: Pew Research Center for People &
the Press telephone survey of 1,500 U.S.
adults, September 2010; margin of error:
+/-3 percentage points
Graphic: Pat Carr

Today, Americans with different backgrounds and views remain divided over the issue of gun control. This chart shows the results of a Pew poll on gun control conducted in September 2010.

murder rate made a steep assent during the crack cocaine boom of the late 1980s and early 1990s. In 1991, the murder rate hit 10 per 100,000—just where it had been in 1933. A much-heralded decline in violent crime, including murder, began in 1994.

In the late 1990s, the trend appeared to be reversing.[5] While violent crime by itself continues to decline, the FBI reports that its "Crime Index" category of violent crimes and serious property crimes—"murder, forcible rape, robbery, aggravated assault, burglary, larceny-theft, and motor vehicle theft"—did increase in 2001 by 2.1 percent when measured in absolute numbers, and by 0.9 percent when measured as a rate per 100,000 inhabitants.[6] In 2008, the five-year violent crime trend shifted again, seeing a high of 1.42 million offenses in 2006, with numbers dropping in 2008 to 1.38 million. While these numbers are higher than the 2004 number of offenses (1.36 million), it is still 3.1 percent below 1999 levels.[7]

Although the fluctuations of the murder and violent crime rates have confounded police and policy makers, they help gun-control advocates refute the argument that increased gun ownership reduces crime. During periods of nationally rising crime rates, though, criminologist John Lott conducted research that he believes shows that increased access to concealed weapons could reduce certain kinds of crime.[8] Gun-control advocates, however, say that Lott's research does not hold up during periods of nationally *falling* crime rates. The antigun Violence Policy Center also claimed when Lott's study came out that the source funding for Lott's University of Chicago fellowship, the John M. Olin Foundation, had continuing close links to its founder's company, the Olin Corporation. The Olin Corporation owns Winchester Ammunition, which the VPC identifies as the largest U.S. producer of ammunition. Lott replied that the charge of association was false, and he persuaded the Associated Press to issue, in his words, "a partial correction stating that the Olin Foundation and Olin Corporation are separate organizations."[9]

A 1999 Brady Center study of FBI statistics from 1992 to 1998 also refuted Lott: In states that make it hard for citizens to carry concealed weapons, the violent crime rate fell by an average of 30 percent. In states that allow easy access to concealed weapons, the violent crime rates dropped by much less, just 15 percent. Nationally, violent crime fell by 25 percent.[10]

International comparisons show the benefits of strong gun control.

Ever since the debate over gun control ignited during the 1960s, advocates have pointed to low firearm-related murder rates in countries such as Japan and the United Kingdom, which have strong gun-control policies. In Denmark, where guns are restricted to use for hunting, the homicide rate is one-fifth as high as in the state of Ohio, even though the two regions share similar rates of injury from assault. By comparison, the majority of U.S. homicides are committed with some kind of firearm—and three-fourths of those involve handguns. U.S. civilians own an estimated 283 million guns—approximately 97 guns for every 100 people.[11] In fact, the deadly relationship between handgun ownership and high crime is especially highlighted when U.S. statistics are compared with those of countries that minimize access to handguns. According to data from the National Center for Health Statistics, the U.S. firearms death rate in 1995 was 13.7 per 100,000; in Canada, it was 3.9 per 100,000; in Australia, it was 2.9 per 100,000; and in England and Wales, it was 0.4 per 100,000.

Advocates have been criticized for using studies that compare different countries without considering cultural differences—other than attitudes toward gun control—that could account for the differences in homicide rates. A novel study released in the 1980s sought to rectify this problem by comparing individual cities that shared many characteristics save one: gun control. The study compared Seattle, Washington, and Vancouver, in the Canadian province of British Columbia. The cities bear remarkable similarities in terms of cultural resources, diversity, and climate. They were, however, very different in one respect: Seattle had few gun controls, and Vancouver had many. A comparison of robberies, burglaries, assaults, and homicides in both cities from 1980 through 1986 showed that although assault rates were only slightly higher in Seattle than in Vancouver, the rate of assault involving firearms was seven times higher in Seattle. The risk of death from homicide was far higher in Seattle than in Vancouver. The additional risk was explained by a nearly 500 percent higher chance of being murdered with a handgun in Seattle. Rates of homicide involving weapons other than guns were not substantially different in the two cities. The study concluded that gun control can reduce homicide significantly.[12]

Tougher enforcement of existing laws will not work.

Gun-rights groups have repeatedly argued that existing U.S. gun laws are ignored and that part of the solution to gun violence is stricter enforcement of existing laws. They urge the imposition of harsher penalties for violent crimes and crimes committed with firearms. Acknowledging that some laws could be better enforced, gun-control advocates counter that all punishments address criminals only *after* they have committed crimes and note that penalties and stiff sentences do nothing to keep guns off the streets in the first place.

The initiatives proposed by advocates of gun control fall into three main categories: limiting access, tracking ownership, and banning some or all firearms. How would this be accomplished? Background checks on buyers in all sales and transfers of firearms would keep dangerous weapons out of dangerous hands. Since the passage of the Brady Act in 1993, hundreds of thousands of felons and other ineligible buyers have been blocked from purchasing guns. The Brady Act—officially, the Brady Handgun Violence Prevention Act[13]—requires an instant background check on all purchases from licensed gun dealers. Sales through unlicensed dealers, though, such as in friendly transfers and at gun shows, do not require a background check. This so-called secondary market accounts for as much as

40 percent of U.S. firearm sales. Gun-control advocates say convicted killers are finding these cracks in the system and walking away armed.[14]

Gun-control advocates have struggled to respond to arguments that gun laws won't affect secondary or illegal gun markets. Their standard reply is that gun laws will reduce the availability of guns in general, thus limiting the number of arms that trickle into the black market. Critics say these advocates need to better address the question of how to enforce gun control in environments controlled by people who make their living by breaking the law.

The success of the Brady Act illustrates the benefits of legislation.

James S. Brady served as President Ronald Reagan's press secretary beginning in January 1981. His career was interrupted on March 30, 1981, when John Hinckley, a mentally disturbed 25-year-old man, emerged from a crowd and fired at the president with a .22-caliber revolver he had purchased five months earlier for $29 at Rocky's Pawn Shop in Dallas, Texas. Reagan, Brady, and two law enforcement officers were hit. Brady was seriously injured with a gunshot wound to the head and became dependent on a wheelchair. The incident inspired Brady and his wife, Sarah, to become involved in the gun-control movement. Working with the pro-gun-control group Handgun Control Incorporated, now the Brady Center to Prevent Gun Violence, the couple began lobbying for legislation that would require longer background checks on all people who want to purchase firearms. Sarah Brady was named chairwoman of the center in 1991.

Progress was slow, but on November 30, 1993, President Bill Clinton signed the Brady Act into law. The law, which took effect on February 28, 1994, required a five-day waiting period and background check on all handgun purchases through licensed dealers. Today the background check is conducted as part of all retail gun purchases. At the time the law passed, 32

James Brady, who was injured by an assassin's bullet during an attempt on President Ronald Reagan's life in 1981, has become an active supporter of gun-control measures. With his wife, Sarah, he founded the Brady Center to Prevent Gun Violence. The Brady Handgun Violence Prevention Act, better known as the Brady Act, was named in his honor.

states had no system for background checks. In these states, felons could be cleared to purchase a firearm simply by signing a statement swearing that they had never been convicted of a felony. Although store owners kept these paper forms on file, the statements were rarely revisited or double-checked. Gun-control advocates call this the "lie and buy" loophole: one just lies about one's past and buys a gun.

Gun-control groups have presented research that they claim shows an immediate impact from the Brady Act on gun trafficking and gun violence. An analysis of FBI crime statistics released by the Brady Center presents evidence that the Brady Act has led to a reduction in the use of firearms in robberies and assaults, possibly preventing thousands of deaths. The study concluded that during the four years after the law passed, between 1994 and 1998, an estimated 9,368 fewer people died than expected because the percentage of robberies and assaults committed with firearms was declining. The number of aggravated assaults committed with a firearm has since fallen by 31.4 percent. The number of robberies committed with a firearm since 1994 has fallen by 33.7 percent. In addition, the number of all murders fell 23.4 percent, whereas the number of murders committed with a firearm fell 29 percent. According to the

THE LETTER OF THE LAW

The Brady Act

The Gun Control Act was amended in 1993 by the Brady Act, which provided for, on an interim basis, a five-day waiting period on handgun sales by licensed dealers and manufacturers [18 U.S.C. 922(s)]. The waiting period is designed to give state and local law enforcement officials a chance to perform a criminal records check on the purchaser before the gun is sold. The five-day waiting period provisions of the Brady Act expired in November of 1998 and were replaced with a national instant-check system for all firearms sales [18 U.S.C. 922(t)].

Department of Justice, the Brady Act has prevented 1.8 million criminals and other restricted persons from purchasing a gun from a licensed dealer.[15]

Bans on assault weapons help to control guns that are inappropriate for civilian use.

The Brady Center began as Handgun Control Incorporated, a group focused on limiting access to handguns, the weapons responsible for Brady's injury in 1981 and for the deaths of thousands of U.S. citizens every year. In 1989, however, a new tragedy refocused the nation's attention on a threat from a different kind of firearm: the assault weapon.

In January 1989, Patrick Purdy, a mentally disturbed drifter, opened fire on children in an elementary school playground in Stockton, California. He killed 5 children and injured 29. Purdy was armed with a Chinese-made semiautomatic rifle, a 7.62-mm AKM-56S with a detachable 30-round magazine. Although the gun had been legally imported, it bore a remarkable resemblance to banned Chinese and Soviet AK-47 assault rifles. The massacre touched off a flurry of support for laws that would ban or restrict ownership of so-called assault weapons—semiautomatic firearms modeled after military weapons designed to fire large numbers of bullets in just a few seconds. Such weapons not only have little sporting or hunting utility but also did not exist during the drafting of the Constitution. Because the Framers hardly anticipated the introduction of weapons of such power and lethality, advocates say, assault weapons should be available only for the national defense.

Following this murder spree, legislation passed first in California, but the bill was widely regarded as a "quick fix" without the substance to force real change. National attention soon followed, but it was not until several years later that a federal assault weapons ban passed. The federal law was included in the Violent Crime Control and Law Enforcement Act of 1994, which Clinton signed into law on September 13, 1994.

Police groups offered broad support for the ban. Although there are no good statistics on the numbers of assault weapons used in crimes, police across the United States in the 1980s reported—and Clinton noted in a 1994 speech at the Ohio Peace Officers Training Academy[16]—that semiautomatic assault weapons had become the "weapon of choice"

Some "Assault Weapon" Characteristics

The Brady Center cites the following features as characteristic of assault weapons:

- *A large-capacity ammunition magazine*, which enables the shooter to continuously fire dozens of rounds without reloading. Standard hunting rifles are usually equipped with no more than three- or four-shot magazines.

- *A folding stock* on a rifle or shotgun, which makes guns easier to conceal.

- *A pistol grip* on a rifle or shotgun, which facilitates firing from the hip, allowing the shooter to spray-fire the weapon. A pistol grip also helps the shooter stabilize the firearm during rapid fire or when firing from the ground, and makes it easier to shoot assault rifles one-handed.

- *A barrel shroud*, which is designed to cool the barrel so that the firearm can shoot many rounds in rapid succession without overheating. It also allows the shooter to grasp the barrel area to stabilize the weapon, without incurring serious burns, during rapid fire.

- *A (threaded) barrel* designed to accommodate one of the following:

  (1) *a flash suppressor*, which makes firearms less visible at night and provides stability during rapid fire, helping the shooter maintain control of the firearm;

  (2) *a silencer*, which muffles the sound of gunfire and is rarely used outside of crime; or

  (3) *a bayonet*.

Source: Brady Campaign to Prevent Gun Violence website. http://www.bradycampaign.org.

for drug traffickers, gangs, and paramilitary extremist groups. Before the federal government banned many types of assault weapons in 1994, the ATF estimated that about 1 percent of about 200 million guns in circulation were assault weapons. In comparison, 8 percent of the gun-tracing requests filed at that time by police involved assault weapons.[18] This suggests that assault weapons are used in crimes more than non-assault weapons.

The assault weapons law banned the production and importation of certain semiautomatic rifles, pistols, and shotguns, as well as close copies that retained two or more specific elements of the prohibited models. It also outlawed magazine cartridges that hold more than 10 rounds of ammunition. Firearms and magazines already in the public's possession were excluded from the ban, as were weapons manufactured for police or military use. The bill bans by name the manufacture of 19 different weapons, including the Israeli Uzi, the Intratec TEC-9, and revolving cylinder shotguns such as the ominously named Street Sweeper and Striker 12.

The bill also bans "copies" or "duplicates" of any of the named weapons. Without banning copies, lawmakers would have created an easy way for manufacturers to copy existing assault weapons and sell the copies legally. Despite this wording, some manufacturers have produced close reproductions of banned assault weapons with one or two modifications in an attempt to work around the letter of the law.

The assault weapons ban, however, does not apply to all guns; those designed for use in hunting and recreational activities are not affected. Addressing concerns that weapons would be taken away from hunters and sporting shooters, the law specifically protects 670 types of hunting rifles and shotguns. The list is not exhaustive, and a gun does not have to be on the list to be protected.

Opponents of the assault weapons ban felt that the guns were being targeted because of design features that only *appear* menacing and that these features are really no more dangerous than are those of any other type of firearm. The bill's authors contend that the menacing features—such as silencers, folding stocks, and bayonets—really do make the weapons more dangerous. Such additions are designed for military combat, they say, and make it easier for the user to kill more people in less time. Gun-control advocates say the ban acknowledges the difference between semiautomatic rifles used for sports and hunting and "assault weapons" designed with military use in mind. Semiautomatic hunting rifles are designed to be fired from the shoulder, and their effectiveness depends on the accuracy of a precisely aimed projectile; semiautomatic assault weapons are designed to maximize lethal effects through a rapid rate of fire. They are spray-fired from the hip, so a shooter can control the weapon with one hand while firing a large amount of ammunition.

It was the gun-rights lobby that pressed the above arguments and pressured Congress to not renew the assault weapons ban when it expired in the fall of 2004. Despite President George W. Bush's support of the ban and the support of every national law enforcement agency, the ban was allowed to lapse. Gun-control organizations argue that the ban had led to a reduction in assault weapons on the streets and being used in crimes, and that it should be reinstated.[18]

Loopholes make existing gun laws ineffective.

On April 20, 1999, Dylan Klebold and Eric Harris opened fire on their classmates and teachers at Columbine High School in Jefferson County, Colorado. The two 17-year-old boys were armed with homemade bombs, a semiautomatic carbine, a semiautomatic pistol, and two sawed-off shotguns. They killed 12 students and one teacher and injured nearly two dozen others before committing suicide. Robyn Anderson, an 18-year-old friend of the two students, had purchased two of the four weapons used in the massacre, no questions asked, from private

54 GUN CONTROL

sellers at the Tanner Gun Show near Denver. Had a background check been required, Anderson later said, she never would have made the purchase.

It is difficult to find statistics on gun control in the United States. Many existing laws are so fraught with loopholes, advocates say, that their effectiveness is impossible to measure. The gun show loophole may be the most notorious. Gun shows were originally fairs put on to display new models and showcase rare curios. In the 1960s and 1970s, as the firearm industry expanded and gun ownership increased, the gun show became a popular venue for simply selling firearms. The 2,000 to 5,000 gun shows

THE LETTER OF THE LAW

The Assault Weapons Ban

The federal assault weapons ban or semiautomatic assault weapons ban is Title XI, subtitle A, of the Violent Crime Control and Law Enforcement Act of 1994. It is formally known as the Public Safety and Recreational Firearms Use Protection Act, and was signed by President Bill Clinton on September 13, 1994.

The assault weapons ban made it a federal crime to possess, sell, or give away an assault weapon. Assault weapons manufactured before the law went into effect were "grandfathered," which means the new ban does not apply to those weapons. The law required that assault weapons manufactured after the ban was enacted be stamped with their date of manufacture.

The law defines assault weapons in a variety of ways, affecting more than 175 firearms in all. It takes great care to mention many by name:

> [A]ny of the firearms, or copies or duplicates of the firearms in any caliber, known as: Norinco, Mitchell, Poly Technologies Avtomat Kalashnikovs (all models); Action Arms I.M.I. UZI and Galil; Beretta AR-70 (SC70); Colt AR-15; Fabrique Nationale FN-FAL/LAR, and FNC; SWD M-10, M-11, M-11/9, and M-12; Steyr AUG; Intratec TEC-9, TEC-DC9, and TEC-22; and revolving cylinder shotguns, such as (or similar to) the Street Sweeper and Striker 12. . . .

Other varieties are not named but are described scrupulously:

held each year in the United States began to attract those seeking to buy guns in anonymity.[19] Even under the Brady Act, which requires licensed gun dealers to run background checks on all sales, unlicensed dealers can sell firearms at gun shows, and in 32 states background checks are not required. Gun-control activists believe the gun shows make it easier for guns to end up in the hands of unqualified owners. Sales by unlicensed dealers, in addition to not being subject to background checks, pose a problem for law enforcement. These purchases are nearly impossible to trace because no records are kept of the sale. Several versions of bills requiring background checks on private

- A semi-automatic rifle that has an ability to accept a detachable magazine and has at least two of the following: a folding or telescoping stock; a pistol grip that protrudes conspicuously beneath the action of the weapon; a bayonet mount; a flash suppressor or threaded barrel; and a grenade launcher.

- A semi-automatic pistol that has an ability to accept a detachable magazine and has at least two of the following: an ammunition magazine that attaches to the pistol outside of the pistol grip; a threaded barrel capable of accepting a barrel extender, flash suppressor, forward handgrip, or silencer; a shroud that is attached to, or partially or completely encircles, the barrel and that permits the shooter to hold the firearm with the nontrigger hand without being burned; a manufactured weight of 50 ounces [1.4 kilograms] or more when the pistol is unloaded; and a semiautomatic version of an automatic firearm.

- A semi-automatic shotgun that has at least two of the following: a folding or telescoping stock; a pistol grip that protrudes conspicuously beneath the action of the weapon; a fixed magazine in excess of five rounds; and an ability to accept a detachable magazine.

This law was allowed to lapse in 2004 and has yet to be renewed by Congress, despite pressure from many groups, including most national police organizations.

and gun show firearms sales have previously been proposed to Congress without much success. Gun-control advocates are hoping for greater success in the future.[20]

Guns make homes more dangerous.

When a gun is used in self-defense, the potential victim's chances of staying alive are usually increased, according to gun-control opponents. What these opponents do not take into account is the fact that victims often do not have time to reach their firearms during an attack. More important, advocates argue, is that guns kept at home for self-defense are more likely to be used in a suicide, accidental death, or homicide than in protecting the owner. Very few murders are the result of a burglary attempt or other felony. Rather, most homicides result from arguments, often among or between people who know each other. Approximately a third of all female murder victims considered in a 2005 Bureau of Justice Statistics (BJS) study had been killed by someone the victims had known.[21]

Gun-control advocates say that by encouraging people to buy handguns for self-defense, the gun industry is perpetrating a dangerous fearfulness, one that causes more deaths than it saves. John Sugarmann notes:

> This spiral of violence—buying handguns to protect ourselves from other people with handguns—fuels gun death and injury in the United States. This is because the handgun bought for self-protection is far more likely to be used against the owner or someone known to the owner—in a homicide (usually as the result of an argument), a suicide, or an unintentional shooting—than in legitimate self-defense.[22]

Gun-control advocates believe that guns in the home pose more risks than they avoid. Keeping a gun at home increases the risk of being murdered by a family member or close friend by nearly three times. In addition to increasing the risk of homicide, guns in the home can increase the risk of suicide: Guns were two times more likely to be found in the homes of adolescents who committed suicide than in the homes of those who unsuccessfully attempted suicide. Some research has shown that suicide is nearly five times more likely in homes with firearms.[23]

Between 1980 and 1992, suicide rates increased among young people between the ages of 10 and 19, as well as among young African-American men and among elderly men of all races. Firearms accounted for 77 percent of the increase in suicides in that same period and were disproportionately responsible for the increases among youths and the elderly. In line with historical precedent, western states had the highest rates of suicide. Firearms accounted for many of the geographic differences in suicide rates and explained much of the increase in several states.

Despite myths that gun violence is only an issue in cities, studies have found that guns kill just as many people in rural areas as they do in urban areas. While homicides involving guns are more prevalent in cities, gun accidents and suicides involving a firearm are more prevalent in rural areas, thus equalizing the number of gun deaths. As Dr. Michael Nance, the author of one study, explains, "[These studies] debunk the myth that firearm death is a big-city problem. . . . This is everyone's problem."[24]

Concealed weapons mean concealed risk.

Many of the events that catalyze renewed interest in gun control become tools for both sides in the debate. The case of Bernhard Goetz is such an example. His story proves that it can be hard to differentiate between aggression and self-defense.

On December 22, 1984, four black teenagers approached Goetz, who is white, on a New York City subway and asked for money. The 37-year-old Goetz, an electrical engineer, had been mugged twice before, and the boys were holding screwdrivers. Goetz, believing he was about to be mugged again, took a silver-plated .38-caliber revolver from his coat and shot and wounded all four of them. Goetz fled but surrendered to police in Concord, New Hampshire, where he confessed to the shooting and to having acted "viciously and savagely." Goetz admitted to police that he told one of the men he shot, Darrell Cabey, "You don't look so bad. Here's another," and shot him again, in the spine, crippling the youth for life. Arguing that he had acted in self-defense, Goetz was later acquitted by a jury on charges of attempted murder and assault. He was sentenced to an eight-month jail term for possessing a concealed gun without a permit.

The Goetz case became international news. Goetz was called "the Subway Vigilante." In an era of rampant crime, some people thought he was a hero for having defended himself. Others thought he was a violent menace who was motivated by fear and racism. Gun-rights groups have continued to champion Goetz as a model for the campaign to liberalize concealed weapons laws. Gun-rights groups believe he is living proof of the value of carrying firearms for self-protection. Given the very real danger of violent crime, they say, Goetz not only saved his own life but may also have struck fear in the hearts of criminals. Gun-control advocates, however, see a warning in his story: If people are allowed, or encouraged, to carry guns at all times, they argue, average people who are afraid, racist, angry, or intoxicated would be more likely to gun down the people around them.

Summary

The United States has a notoriously high rate of handgun deaths, for which many gun-control supporters blame permissive gun-ownership laws. Other countries with stricter gun laws have lower gun-death rates. The trouble in the United States is not with lax enforcement of existing laws, as gun-rights groups suggest; in fact, restrictions in effect now have too many loopholes. The Brady Act's background-check requirement has had some crime-reducing effects, and so has the federal assault weapons law, but these still do not prevent criminals from buying guns informally or at gun shows. Meanwhile, gun-control advocates argue that keeping weapons for self-defense is actually dangerous to the gun owner's own household. They say the mentality of preparation for violent self-defense makes nobody safer and causes a continuing cycle of violence.

Gun Control Does Not Prevent Crime

Almost everyone has heard the NRA mantra "Guns don't kill people—*people* kill people." The idea that guns themselves do not cause gun violence is a fundamental element of the argument against gun control. Most gun owners never use their weapons in crimes, and only a small fraction of guns are used illegally.[1] Despite a mostly steady increase in gun ownership during the twentieth century, crime rates went up and down. With thousands of gun laws that are already unenforced, gun-rights advocates ask what good it will do to pass more. The idea is this: Easy access to guns is not the driving force behind crime. There must be something else.

Guns are not the reason for crime.
Many critics of gun control believe guns have very little to do with the unusual number of violent deaths in the United

States. They direct the public's attention instead to changes in American society—the decline in religious observance, the erosion of traditional family values, and the prevalence of violence in movies and music. Opponents of gun control say the key to reducing crime lies in the laws that already exist, including drug and gun laws, and point to the 20,000-plus gun laws on the books in states and municipalities that are underenforced. By increasing enforcement, they say, police and prosecutors could reduce crime *without* the added confusion of more legislation. In this analysis, they often use successful crime crackdowns in New York and other major cities in the 1990s as examples.

New York has the oldest handgun-licensing law in the United States: the Sullivan Act of 1911. Nonetheless, the city had one of the highest violent crime rates in the country from the 1960s through the 1990s. In the mid-1990s, the New York City Police Department began a massive law enforcement push that focused on eliminating "quality of life" crimes, such as graffiti and loitering; limiting the number of vendors selling pornography; and cracking down on drug crimes, believing that by cracking down on smaller issues would lead to greater reductions in violent crimes. Gun-control opponents note that it was good police work and the enforcement of existing laws—not the creation of additional ones—that reduced crime in New York City.

Another way to look at the impact of better enforcement is to examine crime rates in states where increased enforcement has led to higher prison populations. Between 1980 and 1994, the 10 states with the largest increases in prison population experienced a drop in violent crime by an average of 13 percent, whereas the 10 states with the smallest increases in prison population experienced an average 55 percent increase in violent crime.[2]

Gun-control opponents also point to high crime rates in cities and states that have taken extreme measures to limit access to firearms. Their conclusion is that the controls, although onerous, had little effect on crime. The NRA Web

U.S. guns: Opinion and laws

How public opinion on stricter gun laws has dropped over the past 20 years and how gun laws vary by state:

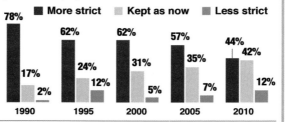

- In general, do you feel that the laws covering the sale of firearms should be:

■ **More strict**   ■ **Kept as now**   ■ **Less strict**

	1990	1995	2000	2005	2010
More strict	78%	62%	62%	57%	44%
Kept as now	17%	24%	31%	35%	42%
Less strict	2%	12%	5%	7%	12%

Background checks Federal and state laws in 49 states* and the District of Columbia require them for firearm buyers

Firearm rights
■ States with provisions in their constitutions to give citizens right to keep, bear arms

R.I. ■
Conn. ■
Del. ■

Mental health
■ Requires reporting of buyer's mental health to FBI criminal background check system

Conn ■

Waiting period
■ Required on gun purchases; includes D.C.

R.I. ■
Conn. ■

Ban assault weapons
■ Prohibits ownership of assault weapons; includes D.C.

Conn. ■

*Vt. has no state law requiring background checks of gun purchasers

Source: Legal Community Against Violence, Brady Center to Prevent Gun Violence. Gallup polls of 1,025 adults, 1990-2010; Margin of error: +/-4 percentage points
Graphic: Melina Yingling, Judy Treible

© 2011 MCT

This chart shows how U.S. public opinion on gun control changed between 1990 and 2010. The maps indicate the states with various gun laws.

site points to efforts in Washington, D.C.; Chicago; New York; Maryland; and California. Washington, D.C., banned handgun sales in 1977, as did Chicago in 1982. By the early 1990s, the homicide rate had tripled in Washington, D.C., and had doubled in Chicago. Chicago had imposed a registration requirement for handguns in 1968 and nevertheless saw rising handgun-related homicide rates. (The restrictions in both areas were later overturned.)

California, a historical testing ground for gun control, increased the waiting period on handgun sales from five to 15 days in 1975 (the waiting period has since been reduced to 10 days), passed an assault weapons ban in 1989, and imposed a waiting period on rifles and shotguns in 1990. Despite all of these measures, the state's annual homicide rate in 2008 remained higher than the rate for the rest of the country, with 5.8 murders per 100,000 people, compared with the U.S. average of 5.4.[3]

Maryland also has imposed extensive restrictions on firearms ownership, including a waiting period; a gun purchase limit; a ban on cheap, compact, small-caliber guns (often called "junk guns" or "Saturday night specials"); restrictions on some assault weapons; and state regulation of the unlicensed transfers of firearms. Nevertheless, the state's homicide rate is, on average, 46 percent higher than the rate for the rest of the country.

According to the NRA, the combined homicide rate for the six jurisdictions with the most restrictive firearms policies—California, Illinois, Maryland, New Jersey, New York, and Washington, D.C.—is 23 percent *higher* than the rate for the rest of the country. In the view of the NRA, the relationship between high murder rates and strong gun control in these states is clear: Gun control does nothing to prevent crime and may even encourage it.

The NRA also contests assertions by gun-control advocates that the major gun laws of the twentieth century—the Brady Act, the assault weapons ban, and the Gun Control Act of 1968—measurably reduced crime rates.[4] Until the passage

THE LETTER OF THE LAW

The Gun Control Act of 1968

The Gun Control Act of 1968 was pushed through Congress in response to the political assassinations of Dr. Martin Luther King Jr. and presidential candidate Senator Robert F. Kennedy that year. The main goal of the GCA was to create categories of "prohibited purchasers," groups of people not legally entitled to possess firearms because of age, criminal background, or incompetence. The prohibited groups include convicted felons, fugitives from justice, illegal-drug users or addicts, minors, anyone adjudicated mentally defective or having been committed to a mental institution, anyone dishonorably discharged from the military, illegal immigrants, and anyone having renounced U.S. citizenship. The law also established a system for licensing dealers, manufacturers, and distributors. In addition, the law:

- Requires serial numbers on all firearms.

- Prohibits the interstate sale of firearms.

- Requires handgun purchasers to buy their guns in the state in which they reside. (Today, long guns may be purchased from gun dealers in any state, regardless of purchaser's state of residence.)

- Sets minimal ages for firearms purchasers: Handgun purchasers must be at least 21. Long gun purchasers must be at least 18.

- Prohibits the importation of nonsporting weapons such as Saturday night specials, some semiautomatic assault rifles, and certain military weapons.

- Bans mail-order sales of firearms and ammunition.

- Sets penalties for use of firearms in crimes of violence or drug trafficking.

- Prohibits importation of foreign-made military surplus firearms.

- Prohibits the sale and manufacture of new fully automatic civilian machine guns.

- Prohibits the sale of parts or "conversion kits" used to make semiautomatic firearms fully automatic.

of the Brady Act and the federal assault weapons ban, the Gun Control Act of 1968 was the nation's most extensive gun-control legislation. The GCA required gun manufacturers and dealers to obtain licenses and prohibited certain groups, such as felons and people with diminished mental capacity, from purchasing guns. The NRA quotes statistics from the years before and after the GCA that show that crime rates were lower before the bill went into effect. The national homicide rate was 50 percent higher, on average, during the five years *after* the law than during the five years before it. Ten years later, the rate was, on average, 81 percent higher.

Gun-control advocates claim that the 1993 Brady Act, which required background checks and waiting periods for gun purchases, has reduced violent crime and murder rates. Critics respond with statistics, such as a study published in the *Journal of the American Medical Association*, which negate the impact of the new law. In August 2000, the journal reported that states implementing waiting periods and background checks did "not [experience] reductions in homicide rates or overall suicide rates."[5]

Gun control puts guns into the hands of criminals.

Another major tenet of the anti-gun-control argument is that gun control will limit only law-abiding citizens' access to guns. Increased regulations, it is said, may in fact catalyze the formation of a black market for guns, increasing the availability of firearms that are unchecked by the gun-control system. An apt historical comparison can be found in the surge of bootlegging and illegal saloons, or speakeasies, during the 1920s and early 1930s, when the Eighteenth Amendment to the Constitution prohibited the manufacture, sale, and distribution of alcohol. Gun-control proposals would erect a series of barriers to gun ownership: waiting periods, background checks, licensing tests, and paperwork for registration. Although responsible gun users struggle with new bureaucratic hurdles, critics say, it will be nearly impossible to make *criminals* comply. If only criminals and police have guns, gun-control opponents argue, cities and suburbs will become much more dangerous. Average people, without access to guns, will be more vulnerable than they are today.

There is also a potential problem with size and scope: With more than 220 million firearms in circulation, gun-rights groups say it would be almost impossible to significantly reduce the number of guns that can enter the black market. Why is that? Because gun-control laws affect only *legal* sales. As an estimated 80 percent of firearms used in crimes are traded through illegal or unregulated means, control opponents say, stricter laws enforced on legal markets will ensure that only criminals have access to guns.

International comparisons are misleading.

Gun-control advocates often cite the low rates of crime in certain countries that enforce strict gun-control laws, such as Great Britain, Italy, and Japan. Gun-control opponents counter with statistics from Switzerland, Israel, and Norway. Gun ownership is high among the last three nations, where gun-related crime rates are comparable with or lower than those in England, Italy, and Japan. Most Swiss men, as members of the national militia, keep government-issued fully automatic rifles and ammunition in their homes. The Swiss government, which maintains a position of neutrality in international affairs, sees arming its citizenry as a method of protecting against foreign attack.

Gun-control opponents believe that international comparisons not only fail to take into account cultural differences that may influence crime rates but also give too much credit to the role of gun control in limiting crime. The presence of gun-control laws, they say, does not reliably predict whether crime rates are high or low in foreign countries, and so the regulations cannot be relied upon to solve America's problems with crime. Of course, this recalls the central argument that people, not guns, are responsible for crime.

Attorney Don B. Kates, whose work includes Second Amendment issues, wrote:

> In any society, truly violent people are only a small minority. We know that law-abiding citizens do not commit violent crimes. We know that criminals will neither obey gun bans nor refrain from turning other deadly instruments to their nefarious purposes. . . . In sum, peaceful societies do not need general gun bans and violent societies do not benefit from them.[6]

Self-defense reduces crime.

Perhaps the most compelling argument in the debate over gun-control concerns is self-defense. Handgun owners consistently say defense against attackers is the chief reason for their firearms purchases. As U.S. citizens are afraid of being the victims of violent crimes and believe that the police cannot guard against every break-in and assault, many have purchased firearms to protect their families. When would-be victims use a firearm in self-defense, critics of gun-control measures say, fewer crimes are successful. Thus, if gun-control laws prevent people from protecting themselves by reducing access to guns, the laws allow some crimes to occur that might have been prevented had the restrictions not been in place.

Analysts in the anti-gun-control camp have focused on the number of cases in which guns are actually used to stop crimes in action. In statistical studies, it has been shown that when a gun is used in self-defense, the victim's chances of surviving increase. Gun-control opponents such as criminologists Gary Kleck and Marc Gertz have presented statistics showing an estimated 2.5 million defensive uses of firearms each year.[7] This is three to five times the estimated number of violent crimes committed with firearms annually.

Criminologist John Lott took this point a step further, arguing that increased gun ownership may actually reduce crime by serving as a deterrent to criminals. Lott's research measured the effect on crime rates of increased gun ownership and increased access to carrying concealed weapons. He put forward a study that showed how in communities where more people own guns, the rate of violent crime decreases.[8] (This conclusion is controversial because it asserts the exact opposite of what gun-control advocates have maintained for years.)

Gun-control opponents point to such national and local statistics to show how lower crime rates can occur once the government allows citizens greater access to weapons. In 1982, Kennesaw, Georgia, passed an ordinance that required the heads of households, with some exceptions, to keep ammunition and at least one firearm in the house. For the next five years, burglaries declined by 89 percent.[9] Although the ordinance may not have actually increased gun ownership, gun-rights groups say a clear message still rang clear: "[A]ny homeowner confronted during a burglary would almost certainly be armed."[10] Kennesaw proudly celebrated the twenty-fifth anniversary of the law in 2007, with gun-rights advocates cheering how the law has maintained such a low crime rate.[11] Another notable statistic that gun-rights advocates point to is a safety course that taught women in Orlando, Florida, how to use guns in 1966 and 1967. Following that course, rape rates declined by 88 percent. Such a decline has been confirmed by the U.S. Department of Justice. A 1979 study by the Justice Department found that 32 percent of attempted rapes were successful. When the potential victim was armed with a gun or knife, the success rate of attempted rapes dropped to 3 percent.[12]

Concealed weapons help reduce crime.

These studies centered on communities that had liberalized their concealed-weapons laws. Concealed-carry weapons laws (CCWs) allow people to carry guns in public. The NRA began a campaign to pass lenient concealed-carry laws in the 1980s. Some existing laws, the so-called "may issue" laws, allowed police to make the final decision in granting a concealed-weapon per-mit to an applicant who met certain qualifications. The NRA lobbied state legislatures to change the "may issue" laws into "shall issue" laws, which would force police to grant a permit to any applicant who met basic criteria.

In his book *More Guns, Less Crime,* Lott cites statistics from the late 1980s and early 1990s, when rising gun ownership accompanied falling national crime rates. He writes that the states with the largest drops in crime at the time were also the states with the "fastest growing percentages of gun ownership." He argues that in states that have passed more lenient concealed-carry laws, murder and crime rates dropped. According to his review of statistics in all U.S. counties from 1977 to 2005, states that passed concealed-carry laws saw a reduction of 20 percent in their rates of murder, rape by 14 percent, aggravated assault by 13 percent, and robbery by 6 percent.[13] "Many factors influ-ence crime," Lott writes, "with arrest and conviction rates being the most important. However, nondiscretionary concealed-handgun laws are also important, and they are the most cost-effective means of reducing crime."[14]

Lott bases his argument on the logical assumption that criminals take the easiest route possible. If certain crimes, such as armed robbery, become more difficult—perhaps because more citizens are armed—then the criminals will attempt them less frequently. Gun ownership, Lott contends, is therefore a method of deterring crime. "Allowing citizens to carry con-cealed handguns reduces violent crimes," Lott declares. ". . . Mass shootings in public places are reduced when law abiding citizens are allowed to carry concealed handguns."[15]

Gun-rights activists rely on survey data showing that crimi-nals are less likely to break the law if they suspect citizens are armed. According to a Justice Department study, three-fifths of felons polled agreed that "a criminal is not going to mess around with a victim he knows is armed with a gun." Nearly 75 percent of felons polled agreed that "one reason burglars avoid houses when people are at home is that they fear being shot during the crime." Fifty-seven percent of felons polled agreed that "criminals are more worried about meeting an armed victim than they are about running into the police."[16]

"Safety" features are dangerous in their own right.

If self-defense is one of the main reasons for owning a handgun, it follows that anything designed to make guns less accessible would be opposed by gun owners. Therefore, opponents believe that safety precautions, such as storing guns unloaded and using trigger locks, reduce the usefulness of firearms as tools for self-defense. Trigger locks and unloaded storing measures make it much less likely that potential victims would be able to unlock and load their weapons quickly enough to protect themselves during an attack. Opponents also argue that these safety measures reduce the usefulness of firearms as passive crime deterrents. A gun serves as a deterrent, many owners contend, because criminals may fear the consequences of attacking a public that is likely to be armed. By making it harder for citizens to use their weapons, these "safety" precautions could actually make criminals feel less vulnerable when committing crimes. Opponents believe the law should allow gun owners to store their weapons in the most easily accessible fashion possible: loaded and within reach.

Targeted bans are a dangerous step toward restricting freedom.

Since the early 1970s, campaigns have come and gone for targeted bans on Saturday night specials, "cop-killer bullets," "assault rifles," and plastic guns. Activists for gun availability fear that these limited restrictions are merely a means to more prohibitionist bans that target all or most firearms. The NRA and other gun-rights groups believe the ultimate aim of all gun-control policies is the outright prohibition of firearms.

The movement to enact targeted bans on handguns began in the 1970s. A 1972 Senate bill, which ultimately failed, would have restricted the production of Saturday night specials, guns that were inexpensive and likely to be used by criminals. Broader restrictions on handguns were sought in the 1980s, especially after the assassination attempt on President Ronald Reagan. Believing these targeted efforts would eventually lead to a mass movement to ban all guns, the NRA and other groups responded in force. They defended handguns as tools for self-defense. Most people who buy firearms for protection choose handguns. According to research by Kleck, small handguns are probably more often bought by poor people for protection rather than used in crimes. Bans on such guns, Kleck writes, "would have their greatest impact in reducing the availability of defensive handguns to low-income people."[17]

In the late 1980s, the focus turned to assault weapons, which culminated in the passage of the assault weapons ban, part of the Violent Crime Control and Law Enforcement Act of 1994. Gun-rights activists opposed the bill, believing that it would restrict guns in the loosely defined category of assault weapons just because the weapons *look* scary and not because they pose a greater threat. They also suggest that such bans are difficult to define, a criticism they apply to almost all gun-control policies. A definition of a Saturday night special could be as narrow as a detailed quality checklist or as broad as "all handguns shorter than four inches." Assault rifles are even more difficult to define. The military-style design features that characterize such guns do not necessarily make them more dangerous, contends the NRA, which believes it is nearly impossible to come up with an effective legal definition of assault weapons, and therefore the law is a hodgepodge of directed bans that could potentially restrict guns popular for legal hunting and sporting events.

Gun-control opponents also argue that assault weapons, however they are defined, are rarely involved in crimes. This fact, they argue, exposes the political motivations of gun-control advocates. In addition, even banned assault weapons are still relatively easy to purchase because firearms manufacturers flooded the market with extra guns before the ban went into effect. Gun manufacturers also found ways to produce guns with a few modifications that would meet the requirements of the ban.

Summary

Gun-rights advocates argue that there are many reasons for crime other than gun availability, a fact that makes international comparisons misleading. They say restricting guns is not an effective way to fight crime; on the contrary, encouraging gun possession, including the carrying of concealed weapons, can have the effect of discouraging crime. Gun-rights advocates further argue that safety measures such as trigger locks make guns less readily available for self-defense and that limiting a particular kind of gun, such as the "Saturday night special," is a step toward restricting fundamental freedoms.

Manufacturers Should Share in Guns' Costs to Society

In 1999, there were 28,874 gun-related deaths in the United States; in 2000, there were 28,663.[1] These were the first two years in nearly two decades in which the number had fallen below 30,000—a decline too small for most to consider a victory. By 2005, the numbers were back up to 31,000.[2] Gun violence, like all causes of injury and death, has an economic impact on families and government. Gunshot wounds cost thousands of dollars to treat. The average cost of a gun-related crime may be as high as $268,000.[3] Cities, states, and counties often are left with the burden of providing emergency care to victims of gun violence who cannot afford medical attention on their own. Gun violence also necessitates millions more in spending on police, courts, prisons, and school security. The most recent research estimates that, in the aggregate, the direct cost of firearms injuries is more than $100 billion per year.[4]

Guns are consumer products *designed* to injure or kill. Gun-control advocates posit a question: The makers of other dangerous products—cars, drugs, and machinery—are held to strict safety guidelines and must pay when those products prove harmful. Why not gun manufacturers?

There is strong public support for holding manufacturers responsible.

Starting in 1998, Chicago, New Orleans, and other U.S. cities and counties began filing suits against gun manufacturers for damages from the negative effects of gun violence in their communities. Most of the suits have targeted manufacturers and gun sellers, blaming the gun makers for producing and marketing a dangerous product and blaming dealers for distributing the product unethically. The suits rest on the legal concept of liability, the idea that when a person or entity fails in a responsibility or duty to another person or group, that duty can be enforced with a variety of punishments, including monetary damages paid to those who suffer.

The impetus for the dozens of lawsuits against gun manufacturers is often traced to the death of a young boy on the streets of Chicago in 1996. Stephen Young's son was killed by a bullet fired from a speeding car by a reputed gang member. The gunman was wielding a Bryco 9 mm semiautomatic handgun that had been bought along with 40 other weapons during a single purchase in a suburban gun shop. Known as "straw buys," such purchases are organized by middlemen who buy large stocks of weapons from licensed dealers and then resell the guns to criminals who cannot legally purchase firearms.

Stephen Young, along with three other Chicago families, filed suit against gun manufacturers, seeking damages for the loss of their loved ones. The suit alleged malfeasance on the part of the gun industry for designing certain weapons with a criminal's taste in mind, such as short revolvers that can easily be hidden. It accused companies of marketing their products directly to criminals by touting handy attributes, like the TEC-DC9 assault rifle's resistance to fingerprints.

Inspired by Young's suit against the industry, the city of Chicago made its own claim against the industry. On November 12, 1998, the city and Cook County filed a lawsuit against 23 gun manufacturers, 12 gun dealers, and numerous intermediary gun distributors. The lawsuit was based partially on an undercover operation that unearthed a vast network of illegal gun trafficking from less-regulated areas outside Chicago into the inner city, where handguns and assault weapons are strictly limited. Over a three-month period, undercover officers from the Chicago Police Department attempted to purchase weapons from the 12 gun stores around Chicago that had sold the highest numbers of guns traced to crimes in the city. The agents presented store clerks with Chicago identification. It was a clear sign that these "customers" wanted to break the law: Chicago residents are prohibited from purchasing the firearms

THE LETTER OF THE LAW

Gun-Related Federal Offenses

Gun control tends to fall to the purview of individual states, but federal law does step in on a number of points. Gun-related crimes that have been designated as federal offenses include:

- Lying to a licensed dealer in order to buy a gun [18 U.S.C. §922(a)(6)]

- Stealing a gun [18 U.S.C. §§922(u), 924(k), 924(l)], or handling or transporting a stolen gun [18 U.S.C. §922(j)] or a gun whose serial number has been erased [18 U.S.C. §922(k)]

- Selling or giving a gun to anyone under the age of 18 [18 U.S.C. §922(x)], being in possession of a gun in a school zone, regardless of age [18 U.S.C. §922(q)], and being a minor and having a gun, regardless of how it was acquired [18 U.S.C. 922(k)] the agents were attempting to buy. In their interactions with store owners, the agents boasted about the criminal purposes for the weapons: selling the guns to gangs or "settling a score." Nonetheless, they walked away with 171 guns and advice from many dealers on how to avoid federal legal requirements in making the purchases.

Chicago was soon joined by dozens of other cities and states seeking damages from the gun industry for failing to produce and market its products responsibly. The lawsuits—and others—also sought to force industry reform. Gun-control advocates hoped the gun makers would begin making safer guns and endorsing sensible controls. While the cities used a variety of strategies in designing their suits, the cases were built around three main ideas: unsafe gun design, negligent distribution, and deceptive marketing and advertising.

In 2005, the gun manufacturers' lobby won a legislative victory with the passage of the Protection of Lawful Commerce in Arms Act (PLCAA).[5] This act effectively squashed the pending lawsuits against the gun industry by providing special protections for the gun industry, effectively making them immune from lawsuits unless there was a specific design flaw in the gun that made it unsafe, or if criminal activity by the manufacturer was involved. While this stopped many of the lawsuits, it proved a moral victory for proponents of gun control. They saw this legislation as proof that the gun industry could not stand up under the scrutiny of the courts.

In response to this legislation, gun-control advocates accused legislators of protecting the gun industry. While the PLCAA was still before Congress, Kristen Rand of the Violence Policy Center wrote:

This misguided legislation would protect the manufacturers of the assault weapons used in the April 20, 1999, Columbine massacre in Littleton, CO: the TEC-

DC9 assault pistol and the Hi-Point Carbine. Instead of protecting communities from gun violence, Congress is working to protect gun manufacturers' bottom line.[6]

Gun designs often are unsafe.

Many of the lawsuits that were filed before the PLCAA incorporate arguments that gun makers ignored the likely and preventable misuse of their products and failed to make safe weapons. This tactic relied upon state statutes under which well-functioning products can be deemed defective if they are unreasonably dangerous in design. These suits assert that locking systems and "smart gun" technology are available but gun makers choose not to use them. Manufacturers also have been slow to incorporate "magazine disconnect safeties" or "'chamber loaded' indicators," which can notify handlers if a gun is ready to fire ammunition. This tactic followed strategies used in lawsuits against car makers who failed to install seatbelts or airbags. In addition to seeking damages, the lawsuits were aimed at changing designs for future weapon production.

Manufacturers do not monitor the distribution of guns effectively.

The lawsuits also assailed the gun industry for distributing their products negligently, in a manner that jeopardized communities. This tactic addressed the alleged failure of the gun industry to monitor and control the sales practices of distributors and dealers. Lawyers argued that, without any oversight, dealers knowingly sell guns into a secondary market in which legally purchased firearms are resold at street level to criminals and others who cannot legally buy them. The suits accuse the industry of knowing that the guns will filter through to illegal markets. Communities that have filed these suits aim to tighten distribution practices and keep guns out of criminals' hands.

Manufacturers and dealers conceal the danger of guns.

Many of the cities also asserted that the gun industry engaged in deceptive marketing practices. By advancing arguments that guns make homes safer, these suits contend, the gun industry has lied to consumers. Gun-control advocates have long held that a gun is far more likely to kill or injure a household member than an intruder, and a gun's presence in a home greatly increases the chances of a homicide, suicide, or accidental death.

Although most of the lawsuits did not go forward, gun retailers, who were often implicated when cities took manufacturers to court, began to explore their options. In 2002, the world's largest retail chain, Wal-Mart Stores Incorporated, decided to make screenings of gun purchases at its stores more thorough by taking an extra step beyond the federal background-check requirements. The chain, which sells firearms in most of its 2,700 stores, now prohibits sales until potential buyers have been approved by the appropriate federal or state agency. Under Brady Act regulations, a gun sale can proceed if the government fails to finish its background check within three business days. Wal-Mart was immediately criticized by the NRA, which accused the chain of interfering with citizens' Second Amendment rights. NRA spokesman Andrew Arulanandam said the Wal-Mart policy "penalizes law-abiding citizens."[7] Ultimately, under pressure from members who supported Wal-Mart's decision, the NRA decided to work with the chain to improve the background-check system.

Despite the setback that many plaintiffs' experienced after the passage of the PLCAA, some lawsuits are still working their way through the courts. As of early 2011, Gary, Indiana, was one city that was using public-nuisance laws to sue gun manufacturers such as Smith & Wesson and Berretta over the way guns entered the stream of commerce and over certain design issues. The Gary lawsuit survived multiple appeals from the gun manufacturers that claimed the lawsuit should be thrown out under the PLCAA. Unlike the Stephen Young case and others like it, this case was based on a sting by undercover police officers who posed as underage and criminal purchasers of guns in several straw buys from multiple manufacturers.[8]

Summary

Cities and individuals affected by gun violence have brought lawsuits against gun manufacturers, seeking to hold them responsible for the criminal use of their products. From the cities' point of view, gun violence forces them to spend money on health care and other services, and so the companies that make guns available to criminals should help pay for the damage. Principal theories of liability in their complaints have included unsafe design, negligent distribution, and deceptive marketing and advertising. While these lawsuits have been overshadowed by federal laws limiting and often disallowing such suits, some lawsuits have still able to work their way through.

Gun Manufacturers Are Not Responsible for Gun-Related Deaths

Gun manufacturers dismiss liability suits as fundamentally flawed, and argue that they produce a legal product and cannot be expected to control how people use firearms any more than automakers can control how people drive. Industry lawyers have some advantages in designing such a defense. To begin with, gun makers never promised the public that their products were safe. The dangerous and lethal capabilities of guns were always acknowledged and sometimes even trumpeted.

Because the plaintiffs in liability lawsuits have used numerous tactics in arguing their cases, the gun industry had an intellectual advantage, observers say. Its position has always remained the same: Whoever fires a gun bears full liability for whatever may happen. The industry itself cannot hold back the trigger.

Product-liability lawsuits are a common and accepted way of forcing manufacturers to produce safe products. These lawsuits target companies that build products with clear faults (i.e., parts that malfunction and cause injury). Gun industry lobbyists have argued that gun-related deaths, however, have nothing to do with product liability. Guns may have been used negligently or with criminal intent, but the guns themselves cannot be blamed. The gun manufacturers say that going after them distracts from the real problems: crime and social breakdown.

Some suits have attacked the industry for failing to include safety features such as "smart gun" technology that would prevent anyone other than the owner from firing a weapon. Industry lobbyists counter that by noting that such technologies are prohibitively expensive and not yet perfected. Gun-control opponents say expensive "smart gun" technology would prevent poor people from accessing a tool for self-defense. In a *National Review* article, criminologist John Lott writes, "The futuristic guns advocated in the New Orleans suit . . . are far from reliable and will cost $900 when they are finally available."[1] Since 2005, the gun industry has had an additional defense that has all but shut down most legislation: the Protection of Lawful Commerce in Arms Act.

Lawsuits against gun manufacturers threaten a legitimate industry.

Some critics have derided the lawsuits as gold-digging expeditions against law-abiding businesses that contribute to the national economy. Then-Representative Chris John, a Democrat from Louisiana, warned, "Frivolous lawsuits against gun manufacturers jeopardize a legitimate, legal business that is worth billions of dollars to our national economy."[2]

The NRA vehemently opposed the shift in the arena of the gun-control debate from Congress and state legislatures to the courts. In the mid-1990s, the NRA began pushing for legislative protections for gun manufacturers that would have made it illegal for groups of people or municipalities to sue gun makers for product liability. Like other conservative activist groups, the NRA favors legislation over court-set precedent. The group's decision to fight lawsuits with legislation was thus no surprise. Since the first suit was introduced, more than 30 states enacted NRA-backed legislation that prohibits localities from filing lawsuits.

In 2001, the NRA supported the introduction of the PLCAA.[3] The federal legislation was vital to the industry because state bills were not as effective in preventing lawsuits. Jeff Reh, general counsel for Beretta USA, a major American gun manufacturer, gave the following testimony in favor of the federal ban on lawsuits against the industry:

> If the tactic of these lawsuits is allowed to succeed, recourse to the courts can make the legislature superfluous. This violates the Separation of Powers in the Constitution. It also robs the public of their elected voice in government. Regrettably, cases of this type can succeed, not just through a jury verdict, but because of the costs of defending against litigation. Most firearm manufacturers have small revenues and low profit margins. The tyranny of legal costs can and has driven firearm manufacturers into bankruptcy. Lawsuits put money in the pockets of lawyers rather than in the

Who Administers Gun Laws?

Although state and local governments have their own gun ordinances, the responsibility of enforcing federal gun laws rests with the Department of the Treasury. The Bureau of Alcohol, Tobacco, Firearms and Explosives, a subsection of the Treasury, oversees most of the laws; the exception is the exportation provisions of the Arms Export Control Act (AECA), which is the domain of the State Department and U.S. Customs and Border Protection.

On April 15, 2009, an anti-gun-control flag was flown at a gathering held at the state capitol in Phoenix, Arizona. Nearly 10,000 people attended the rally, which was convened to oppose the Obama administration's economic plan but turned into a general anti-Obama rally.

hands of factory workers. Many countries consider domestic firearm production to be a vital national security interest. These lawsuits threaten that resource in the United States.

Begun to advance one narrow point of view, these cases risk a vital industry. If, for example, a single judge or jurors in one city enter a verdict against the industry in the sum of billions of dollars, the cost of purchasing a bond before an appeal can be undertaken could bankrupt even the most substantial company. Rogue juries or individual judges might see such cases as an opportunity to destroy firearm companies and, either unwittingly or without caring, block the means by which U.S. citizens exercise their Second Amendment freedoms of self-defense and self-determination.[4]

Gun manufacturers also argue that the suits are factually flawed in their argument that the industry has failed to establish regulations that keep guns out of dangerous hands. They argue that the sale and distribution of firearms is, in fact, heavily regulated. In 2005, the gun manufacturers won their argument, as Congress passed the PLCAA, which President George W. Bush signed into law. One legal commentator explained, "In particular, the PLCAA bars plaintiffs from suing firearm manufacturers for the negligent or criminal misuse of guns by third parties. It also requires pending lawsuits involving such misuse to be dismissed."[5] This ultimately meant that an individual plaintiff could not sue the gun maker if a criminal used one of their guns to harm the plaintiff, nor could municipalities sue for reimbursement from gun manufacturers for the taxpayers costs of gun violence.[6]

Even with the protections of the PLCAA, the remaining lawsuits expose a possible rift between the gun industry and traditional advocates of the right to bear arms. Unlike the NRA, gun manufacturers may be willing to tolerate limited control policies—such as increasing waiting periods and background checks—in order to ensure a lawsuit-free future and a stable marketplace. Many gun dealers believe they would actually benefit from tighter controls on private sales and transfers at gun shows. Trading tighter restrictions for a reduction in liability might also be a smart move: Some of the civil lawsuits still pending are demanding hundreds of millions of dollars in damages.

Summary

Gun manufacturers and owners' groups argue that lawsuits regarding manufacturer liability are logically flawed because people who misuse guns bear full responsibility for their actions. They also say the suits endanger a legitimate industry. Gun manufacturers have defeated some attempts by cities and individuals to hold them liable for gun violence, and have been successful in persuading many state legislatures and the federal government to pass laws blocking suits of this type. It appears that even with these legislative protections, it is possible that gun manufacturers may be willing to accept some restrictions in exchange for a reduction in liability, but those who support gun owners' rights remain unlikely to compromise.

The Future of Gun Control in the United States

The gun-control debate is far from waning. In fact, Supreme Court decisions in 2008 and 2010 may have made the controversy even more complicated than it was before. With both gun-control and gun-rights advocates claiming these decisions support some of their claims and positions, the new areas of debate are likely to be as controversial as previous ones.

The 2010 Supreme Court decision in *McDonald v. Chicago* further changes the legal landscape for the gun-control debate. Closely following the 2008 decision in *District of Columbia v. Heller*, the Supreme Court explained that the Second Amendment does provide an individual right to own a gun, and that right must be protected by state and local governments as well as the federal government. Justice Samuel Alito wrote in the majority opinion:

In *Heller*, we held that the Second Amendment protects the right to possess a handgun in the home for the purpose of self-defense. Unless considerations of *stare decisis* counsel otherwise, a provision of the Bill of Rights that protects a right that is fundamental from an American perspective applies equally to the Federal Government and the States. We therefore hold that the Due Process Clause of the Fourteenth Amendment incorporates the Second Amendment right recognized in *Heller*.[1]

While gun-rights advocates considered this ruling a victory, other sections of the opinion provided support for gun-control advocates who wish to continue or even further regulate gun ownership. Alito also states in the opinion:

It is important to keep in mind that *Heller*, while striking down a law that prohibited the possession of handguns in the home, recognized that the right to keep and bear arms is not "a right to keep and carry any weapon whatsoever in any manner whatsoever and for whatever purpose." We made it clear in *Heller* that our holding did not cast doubt on such longstanding regulatory measures as "prohibitions on the possession of firearms by felons and the mentally ill," "laws forbidding the carrying of firearms in sensitive places such as schools and government buildings, or laws imposing conditions and qualifications on the commercial sale of arms." We repeat those assurances here. Despite municipal respondents' doomsday proclamations, incorporation does not imperil every law regulating firearms.[2]

Open and Concealed Carry Laws

One area of increasing controversy has to do with laws that permit people to carry guns on their person, either concealed or in the open. As of early 2011, 35 states have "shall issue" laws that require law enforcement agencies to issue concealed-weapons permits to anyone who meets certain minimum requirements. Twelve states have "may issue" statutes that allow law enforcement greater discretion in issuing permits. Of the other states, two do not allow any concealed carrying or weapons, while the other two do not require a permit to carry.[3] Because of the variety of laws, gun-rights activists have spent time and effort on federal concealed-carry legislation, although it has not been approved by Congress.[4]

An even more visible controversy has arisen as some gun advocates have begun openly carrying weapons. This is a far less regulated area, and gun advocates see openly carrying guns as a way of making a statement. They also do so sometimes when they are not allowed to get a concealed-weapons permit. This phenomenon caught the attention of national media when protesters at health care reform forums and rallies began protesting while carrying handguns and rifles.[5]

Where Can Guns Go?

The controversy over how guns can be carried naturally has led to a controversy over *where* guns can be carried. College campuses, public parks, even restaurants and coffee shops have become epicenters for gun-control debates. College campuses have historically been gun-free zones, and most legal scholars agree that these restrictions are likely to remain unaffected by recent Supreme Court rulings. Others, however, point out that there is room for some question in situations where schools are located in urban and suburban areas that have loosely defined boundaries, making it questionable as to where guns would be prohibited.[6]

In 2009, the question of guns in national parks came to the forefront of the gun-control debate. As part of a political compromise to gain passage of a bill to protect credit card holders, an amendment was added that allowed firearms into national parks. Previously guns were only allowed in special circumstances, but the new law allowed guns if the state in which the park was located in allowed them. This meant that the gun-carry requirements would be the same inside and outside of the park.[7]

Public accommodations also are having to confront whether they will allow customers to bring weapons into their

---

QUOTABLE

Starbucks' Position on Open Carry Gun Laws

We recognize that there is significant and genuine passion surrounding the issue of open carry weapons laws. Advocacy groups from both sides of this issue have chosen to use Starbucks as a way to draw attention to their positions.

While we deeply respect the views of all our customers, Starbucks longstanding approach to this issue remains unchanged. We comply with local laws and statutes in all the communities we serve. That means we abide by the laws that permit open carry in 43 U.S. states. Where these laws don't exist, openly carrying weapons in our stores is prohibited. The political, policy and legal debates around these issues belong in the legislatures and courts, not in our stores.

At the same time, we have a security protocol for any threatening situation that might occur in our stores. Partners are trained to call law enforcement as situations arise. We will continuously review our procedures to ensure the highest safety guidelines are in place and we will continue to work closely with law enforcement.

We have examined this issue through the lens of partner (employee) and customer safety. Were we to adopt a policy different from local laws allowing open carry, we would be forced to require our partners to ask law abiding customers to leave our stores, putting our partners in an unfair and potentially unsafe position.

As the public debate continues, we are asking all interested parties to refrain from putting Starbucks or our partners into the middle of this divisive issue. As a company, we are extremely sensitive to the issue of gun violence in our society. Our Starbucks family knows all too well the dangers that exist when guns are used irresponsibly and illegally. Without minimizing this unfortunate reality, we believe that supporting local laws is the right way for us to ensure a safe environment for both partners and customers.

Source: http://news.starbucks.com/article_display.cfm?article_id=332.

establishments or not. California has seen a great deal of controversy in this area, as restaurants such as California Pizza Kitchen and Peet's Tea & Coffee banned guns from their establishments, while Starbucks caused waves with its policy to allow guns in its coffee shops.[8]

More Loopholes Emerge

Other controversies continue to erupt over such issues as how gun-control regulations are implemented and how effective they are. Often, guns have found their way into the hands of people who have no legal right to them. During the summer of 2002, a new problem with Brady Act background checks was exposed. According to a report from the General Accounting Office (now the Government Accountability Office), nearly 3,000 domestic abusers purchased firearms between 1998 and 2001 through a glitch in records check systems.[9] If the FBI is unable to complete the Brady background check within three days, the sale is allowed to proceed. This provision was a compromise measure that helped move the original Brady bill through Congress.

Investigators were forced to track down the abusers and more than 8,000 other prohibited buyers who had been allowed to buy weapons. More than a quarter of the cases involved people convicted of misdemeanor domestic violence offenses. Because of poor bookkeeping practices and other problems, it proved difficult to find such records. The GAO study argues that federal authorities should be given as much as 30 days to research suspicious cases before a sale is approved, noting that a relatively small number of buyers would be affected. Some members of Congress have recommended, in contrast, shrinking the background check time to 24 hours in some cases.

Arming Pilots to Protect Against Terrorism

In the immediate aftermath of the terrorist attacks on September 11, 2001, gun control seemed to fade from public attention. The lawsuits against gun manufacturers were mired in the appeals process. Crime was on the decline. As the administration of President George W. Bush and representatives in Congress sought solutions to protecting domestic security, however, the issue of access to firearms returned to the forefront of the national debate. A coalition of airline pilot unions, members of Congress, and the NRA began clamoring for legislation that would allow airline pilots to carry handguns. A program was created that allows pilots who undergo training to be certified as "federal flight deck officers," allowing them to carry guns onto their planes.[10]

The practice of allowing pilots to carry firearms aboard planes was common until the 1980s, and was not outlawed until July 2001, just months before the 9/11 attacks.[11] (Airline manufacturers say that modern aircraft can function safely despite any decompression caused by bullet holes in the fuselage.) Critics of the measure argue that guns in the cockpit can cause more problems than they solve. They say pilots should be allowed to focus solely on flying their planes, instead of attempting to manage a deadly weapon at the same time. Supporters of the measure counter that trusting pilots with fuel-loaded jetliners is far riskier than arming them with guns. Casting doubt on the reliability of the air marshal program, which places armed government employees on some flights, they say the federal flight deck officers program is the only sure way to protect passengers. However controversial the program may be, the Obama administration, which took office in January 2009, has made it clear that it intends to not only continue this Bush administration–era program, but is seeking funding to expand it.[12]

Progress Is Still Slow

Although surveys consistently show that a majority of U.S. citizens favor some form of increased gun control, the gun-control lobby has yet to achieve any major legislation.[13] The problem seems to be that the general public lacks the commitment and passion for the issue needed to force change. The tens of millions of gun owners in the United States, however, lobby vigorously to ensure their rights. They often are more motivated than gun-control advocates to support their candidates and feed the coffers of their institutions.

Can Safer Storage Reduce Accidents?

Other gun-control advocates, with the support of suburban and urban police, have begun to focus on the issue of safe gun storage. They advocate using trigger locks, devices that make it impossible to pull the trigger without a key. They also urge gun owners to store their firearms in locked cabinets or safes. These safety measures focus on the tragic cases of accidental death when children find and play with their parents' loaded guns. The gun-safety argument has led some people to believe that guns themselves should be designed to be less danger-ous. Although groups such as the NRA oppose proposals that would set safe-storage standards for firearm owners, gun manufacturers have begun to advocate the use of gun locks and similar devices.

Is Compromise Possible?

Social commentators who have no specific interest in limiting or increasing gun control in the United States offer insights that often cannot be found in the literature published by the differing sides. Many urge gun-rights activists and gun-control advocates to compromise. Others encourage both sides to advocate more politically distinct agendas.

Many commentators at both ends of the political spectrum think gun control fails to address the source of the nation's problems with violence and that a full-scale re-evaluation of the nation's culture is needed to fix the broken parts. The columnist and author Anna Quindlen has said, in light of efforts to reduce violence in schools, "There is a lot of talk now about metal detectors and gun control. Both are good things. But they are no more a solution than forks and spoons are a solution to world hunger."[14]

Summary

With the Supreme Court breaking its decades-long silence on the issue of the Second Amendment, new controversies have come up over how to live with these judicial guidelines. Carrying weapons outside the home has led to many new issues, including where concealed weapons and openly displayed weapons should be allowed. Although the 9/11 terrorist attacks might have been expected to have encouraged the public to support further limits on weapons, one result of the attacks was a federal law permitting pilots to be armed for self-defense during flights. There is still talk of campaigning to ban guns entirely, but in the shorter term, safety measures such as trigger-lock requirements appear to have a stronger chance of passing. Meanwhile, commentators speaking at a distance from the gun debate tend to ask whether the culture of violence in the United States is really the problem most in need of the nation's attention.

Beginning Legal Research

The goals of each book in the POINT/COUNTERPOINT series are not only to give the reader a basic introduction to a controversial issue affecting society, but also to encourage the reader to explore the issue more fully. This Appendix is meant to serve as a guide to the reader in researching the current state of the law as well as exploring some of the public policy arguments as to why existing laws should be changed or new laws are needed.

Although some sources of law can be found primarily in law libraries, legal research has become much faster and more accessible with the advent of the Internet. This Appendix discusses some of the best starting points for free access to laws and court decisions, but surfing the Web will uncover endless additional sources of information. Before you can research the law, however, you must have a basic understanding of the American legal system.

The most important source of law in the United States is the Constitution. Originally enacted in 1787, the Constitution outlines the structure of our federal government, as well as setting limits on the types of laws that the federal government and state governments can enact. Through the centuries, a number of amendments have added to or changed the Constitution, most notably the first 10 amendments, which collectively are known as the "Bill of Rights" and which guarantee important civil liberties.

Reading the plain text of the Constitution provides little information. For example, the Constitution prohibits "unreasonable searches and seizures" by the police. To understand concepts in the Constitution, it is necessary to look to the decisions of the U.S. Supreme Court, which has the ultimate authority in interpreting the meaning of the Constitution. For example, the U.S. Supreme Court's 2001 decision in *Kyllo v. United States* held that scanning the outside of a person's house using a heat sensor to determine whether the person is growing marijuana is an unreasonable search—if it is done without first getting a search warrant from a judge. Each state also has its own constitution and a supreme court that is the ultimate authority on its meaning.

Also important are the written laws, or "statutes," passed by the U.S. Congress and the individual state legislatures. As with constitutional provisions, the U.S. Supreme Court and the state supreme courts are the ultimate authorities in interpreting the meaning of federal and state laws, respectively. However, the U.S. Supreme Court might find that a state law violates the U.S. Constitution, and a state supreme court might find that a state law violates either the state or U.S. Constitution.

Not every controversy reaches either the U.S. Supreme Court or the state supreme courts, however. Therefore, the decisions of other courts are also important. Trial courts hear evidence from both sides and make a decision, while appeals courts review the decisions made by trial courts. Sometimes rulings from appeals courts are appealed further to the U.S. Supreme Court or the state supreme courts.

Lawyers and courts refer to statutes and court decisions through a formal system of citations. Use of these citations reveals which court made the decision or which legislature passed the statute, and allows one to quickly locate the statute or court case online or in a law library. For example, the Supreme Court case *Brown v. Board of Education* has the legal citation 347 U.S. 483 (1954). At a law library, this 1954 decision can be found on page 483 of volume 347 of the U.S. Reports, which are the official collection of the Supreme Court's decisions. On the following page, you will find samples of all the major kinds of legal citation.

Finding sources of legal information on the Internet is relatively simple thanks to "portal" sites such as findlaw.com and lexisone.com, which allow the user to access a variety of constitutions, statutes, court opinions, law review articles, news articles, and other useful sources of information. For example, findlaw.com offers access to all Supreme Court decisions since 1893. Other useful sources of information include gpo.gov, which contains a complete copy of the U.S. Code, and thomas.loc.gov, which offers access to bills pending before Congress, as well as recently passed laws. Of course, the Internet changes every second of every day, so it is best to do some independent searching.

Of course, many people still do their research at law libraries, some of which are open to the public. For example, some state governments and universities offer the public access to their law collections. Law librarians can be of great assistance, as even experienced attorneys need help with legal research from time to time.

Common Citation Forms

Source of Law	Sample Citation	Notes
U.S. Supreme Court	*Employment Division v. Smith*, 485 U.S. 660 (1988)	The U.S. Reports is the official record of Supreme Court decisions. There is also an unofficial Supreme Court ("S. Ct.") reporter.
U.S. Court of Appeals	*United States v. Lambert*, 695 F.2d 536 (11th Cir.1983)	Appellate cases appear in the Federal Reporter, designated by "F." The 11th Circuit has jurisdiction in Alabama, Florida, and Georgia.
U.S. District Court	*Carillon Importers, Ltd. v. Frank Pesce Group, Inc.*, 913 F.Supp. 1559 (S.D.Fla.1996)	Federal trial-level decisions are reported in the Federal Supplement ("F. Supp."). Some states have multiple federal districts; this case originated in the Southern District of Florida.
U.S. Code	Thomas Jefferson Commemoration Commission Act, 36 U.S.C., §149 (2002)	Sometimes the popular names of legislation—names with which the public may be familiar—are included with the U.S. Code citation.
State Supreme Court	*Sterling v. Cupp*, 290 Ore. 611, 614, 625 P.2d 123, 126 (1981)	The Oregon Supreme Court decision is reported in both the state's reporter and the Pacific regional reporter.
State Statute	Pennsylvania Abortion Control Act of 1982, 18 Pa. Cons. Stat. 3203-3220 (1990)	States use many different citation formats for their statutes.

Cases and Statutes

United States v. Cruikshank, 92 U.S. 542 (1875)

In this post–Civil War case, the Supreme Court refused to find that a group of white racists in Louisiana had broken the law by "banding together" to violate the rights of two men "of African descent and persons of color," including not only their rights to vote, assemble, and enjoy equal rights and freedoms under the laws, but also specifically their claimed Second Amendment right "to keep and bear arms for a lawful purpose." The Court wrote, "The right . . . of 'bearing arms for a lawful purpose' . . . is not a right granted by the Constitution. Neither is it in any manner dependent upon that instrument for its existence. The Second Amendment declares that it shall not be infringed; but this . . . means no more than that it shall not be infringed by Congress." The NRA sees this language as saying that "the right of the people to keep and bear arms was a right which existed prior to the Constitution." However, the decision's more general effect was to say that victims of organized intimidation could only turn to their state and local governments, not to the federal government, for protection. In the twentieth century, the Supreme Court gradually found that most of the Bill of Rights applies, via the Fourteenth Amendment, to the behavior of state and local officials in addition to the federal government. Together, Congress and the courts made clear that the federal government protects civil rights such as the right to vote and the right to equal protection of the laws. The Court, however, still did not explicitly state whether the Second Amendment applies to state and local official action.

Presser v. Illinois, 116 U.S. 252 (1886)

The Supreme Court upheld the conviction of Herman Presser for riding through the streets of Chicago at the head of a 400-man armed company that did not have government permission to assist in the national defense. The Court stated: "It is undoubtedly true that all citizens capable of bearing arms constitute the reserved military force or reserve militia of the United States as well as of the States, and in view of this prerogative of the general government, as well as of its general powers, the States cannot, even laying the constitutional provision in question [the Second Amendment] out of view, prohibit the people from keeping and bearing arms, so as to deprive the United States of their rightful resource for maintaining the public security, and disable the people from performing their duty to the general government." The NRA argues that this case also suggests the Second Amendment applies to the actions of state and local governments; the Brady Center's Legal Action Project disagrees.

Miller v. Texas, 153 U.S. 535 (1894)

"[D]efendant claimed that the law of the state of Texas forbidding the carrying of weapons, and authorizing the arrest, without warrant, of any person violating such law, under which certain questions arose upon the trial of the case, was in conflict with the second and fourth amendments to the constitution of the United States. . . . We have examined the record in vain, however, to find where the defendant was denied the benefit of any of these provisions, and, even if he were, it is

97

well settled that the restrictions of these amendments operate only upon the federal power, and have no reference whatever to proceedings in state courts."

The National Firearms Act of 1934

This measure imposed a tax on the manufacture and sale of machine guns, silencers, and short-barrel (sawed-off) shotguns and rifles, and made registration of manufacture and importation mandatory; purchase or other transfer required a background check by the FBI and the approval of local officials.

The Federal Firearms Act of 1938

Required annual licensing of dealers and banned the sale of guns to known criminals.

United States v. Miller, 307 U.S. 174 (1939)

The Supreme Court held that the National Firearms Act was not unconstitutional, either as an impingement by the federal government on rights reserved to the states or as a violation of the Second Amendment. A sawed-off shotgun has no "reasonable relation to the preservation or efficiency of a well-regulated militia," and possession of one is not a right guaranteed by the Second Amendment.

Haynes v. United States, 390 U.S. 85 (1968)

The Supreme Court held that a criminal cannot be convicted for failing to register a firearm because of his Fifth Amendment right against self-incrimination—that is, it is illogical to penalize a person who is in unlawful possession of a firearm for not registering that firearm.

The Gun Control Act of 1968

Banned gun ownership by members of many classes of people, including drug addicts, minors, convicted felons, and people with mental illness; required serial numbers on all guns; banned commerce in guns and ammunition through the mail; set the minimum purchase ages of 21 for handguns and 18 for "long guns"; banned the importation of foreign military products, Saturday night specials, and some semi-automatic weapons; required licensed dealers to keep records of transactions and authorized the federal government to inspect those records as well as the dealers' inventories.

United States v. Cody, 460 F.2d 34 (8th Cir. 1972)

A federal appeals court found that ignorance of the law is no excuse for acquiring a firearm from a dealer through intentional false statements, and the federal law banning such actions is constitutional.

United States v. Swinton, 521 F.2d 1255 (10th Cir. 1975)

A federal appeals court ruled that a person not licensed as a dealer in firearms who sells a firearm can be convicted under a state statute even if the sale is not part of a full-time occupation or done for profit.

United States v. Warin, 530 F.2d 103 (6th Cir. 1976), *cert. denied,* 426 U.S. 948 (1976)

A federal appeals court held that the fact that a person is subject, like other citizens of that state, to enrollment in a state militia does not justify that person's possession of a submachine gun. "It is clear that the Second Amendment guarantees a collective rather than an individual right."

The Arms Export Control Act of 1976
This law invests the president with the authority to control the importation and exportation of "defense articles" through permits and licenses, and it prohibits commerce in such articles with "proscribed countries."

United States v. Oakes, 564 F.2d 384 (10th Cir., 1977), *cert. denied,* 435 U.S. 926 (1978)
A federal appeals court affirmed that the Second Amendment does not guarantee the right to possess an unregistered firearm with no proven connection to a state militia, even if the possessor himself is affiliated nominally with a state militia. Neither a Kansas state law specifying that the state militia included all "able-bodied male citizens between the ages of twenty-one and forty-five years" nor the possessor's affiliation with a nongovernmental "militia-type organization" justified possession.

Lewis v. United States, 445 U.S. 55 (1980)
The Supreme Court held that prohibitions contained in the Gun Control Act of 1968 against the possession of firearms by convicted felons were not unconstitutional. The ruling reaffirmed the *Miller* ruling: "[T]he Second Amendment guarantees no right to keep and bear a firearm that does not have 'some reasonable relationship to the preservation or efficiency of a well regulated militia.'"

Quilici v. Village of Morton Grove, 695 F.2d 261 (7th Cir. 1982), *cert. denied,* 464 U.S. 863 (1983)
A federal appeals court upheld the constitutionality of an ordinance banning handgun possession in the city of Morton Grove, Illinois.

The Firearms Owners Protection Act of 1986
Allowed interstate sale of rifles and shotguns between parties who meet in person and comply with the laws of both states. Increased some penalties for criminal sale or use of guns and banned commerce in machine guns by private citizens. This law has been criticized by the Brady Campaign for increasing the number of gun sales without background checks, expanding the "gun show loophole" and making the inspection and prosecution of lawbreaking firearms dealers more difficult.

The Gun-Free School Zones Act of 1990
Generally prohibited the possession and/or discharge of a gun in a school zone; allowed for certain practical exceptions.

United States v. Verdugo-Urquidez, 494 U.S. 259 (1990)
Primarily a Fourth Amendment case, but seen by the NRA as reinforcing the idea that the Second Amendment's use of "the people" refers to an individual right.

United States v. Hale, 978 F.2d 1016 (8th Cir. 1992)
A federal appeals court held that the Second Amendment does not protect individual possession of military weapons. Reaffirmed the power of Congress to regulate trade in firearms as a form of interstate commerce.

The Brady Act of 1993

Required implementation of a system of background checks of prospective purchasers of handguns (in states that had not already passed such legislation). Not
all firearm transfers are affected—only sales by licensed dealers.

The Violent Crime Control and Law Enforcement Act of 1994

Aimed at reducing the trafficking of semiautomatic assault weapons; banned various models. Prohibited gun ownership by anyone under a restraining order for
domestic violence; raised the standards for procuring a license to sell guns; prohibited generally the sale of handguns to minors and any traffic in magazines that
held at least 10 rounds of ammunition.

United States v. Lopez, 514 U.S. 549 (1995)

In a 5-to-4 vote, the Supreme Court struck down the Gun-Free School Zones
Act of 1990 as beyond the limits of congressional power to regulate interstate
commerce.

The Domestic Violence Offender Gun Ban of 1996

Prohibited anyone convicted of a misdemeanor for a domestic offense from owning a firearm.

Printz v. United States, 521 U.S. 898 (1997)

The Supreme Court restricted the application of the Brady Act by finding that the
federal government could not require state and local law enforcement officials to
conduct background checks under the act.

United States v. Emerson, 270 F.3d 203 (5th Cir. 2001) *cert. denied by Supreme Court Order List of June 10, 2002*

A federal appeals court upheld the conviction of a man who illegally possessed a
gun while under a restraining order for domestic violence, but also said the Second Amendment supports an individual right to gun ownership. Supported the
domestic violence law in the case as among the "limited, narrowly tailored specific
exceptions or restrictions" that the Second Amendment could reasonably permit.

United States v. Haney, 264 F.3d 1161 (2001), *cert. denied by Supreme Court Order List of June 10, 2002*

A federal appeals court upheld a law banning private ownership of machine guns.

The Our Lady of Peace Act (HR 4757, 2002)

Passed the House of Representatives in the fall of 2002 amid the sniper serial kill-
ings in the Washington, D.C., area; named for a church that was the site of a dou-
ble murder. Would improve background check mechanisms to make them more
effective in identifying people with criminal records who should not be allowed to
purchase firearms.

District of Columbia v. Heller, 554 U.S. 570 (2008)

The Supreme Court ruled that the Second Amendment protects a citizen's right to
possess a firearm, unconnected to service in a militia, and to use that weapon for
traditionally lawful purposes, including self-defense within the home.

***McDonald v. Chicago*, 561 U.S. ___, 130 S.Ct. 3020 (2010)**
The Supreme Court ruled that the Second Amendment limits state and local governments to the same extent that it limits the federal government.

Terms and Concepts

"a well-regulated militia"
individual right v. collective right
manufacturer liability
assault weapon
Saturday night special
targeted ban

Introduction: The Politics of Gun Control

1 Center For Responsive Politics Web site, *Gun Control: Background.* http://www.opensecrets.org/lobby/background.php?lname=Q12&year=2008

2 Ibid.

3 *United States v. Miller*, 307 U.S. 174 (1939).

4 Ibid.

5 *McDonald v. Chicago*, 561 U.S. ___, 130 S.Ct. 3020 (2010).

6 *Washington, D.C. v. Heller*, 128 S.Ct. 2783 (2008).

7 Susan Schmidt and Ruben Castaneda, "U.S. Adds to Charges in Sniper Shootings; Affidavit Lists Evidence Found in Muhammad's Car," *Washington Post*, October 30, 2002.

8 Robert M. Thompson, Jerry Miller, Martin G. Ols, and Jennifer C. Budden, *Ballistic Imaging and Comparison of Crime Gun Evidence by the Bureau of Alcohol, Tobacco, and Firearms*, report by the National Integrated Ballistic Information Network Program, U.S. Bureau of Alcohol, Tobacco, Firearms and Explosives, May 13, 2002, p. 2.

9 National Rifle Association Institute for Legislative Action Web site, "'Ballistic Fingerprinting'—The Maryland Example: Costing Taxpayers Without Benefiting Law Enforcement." http://www.nraila.org/Issues/FactSheets/Read.aspx?id=97&issue=078.

10 PR Newswire Web site, "Americans Should be Allowed to Have Guns, Say Large Majorities," June 16, 2010. http://www.prnewswire.com/news-releases/americans-should-be-allowed-to-have-guns-say-large-majorities-96456849.html.

Point: Gun Activists Misconstrue the Second Amendment

1 Warren Burger, interviewed on PBS's *MacNeil-Lehrer NewsHour*, December 16, 1991.

2 National Guard Web site, "About the National Guard." http://www.ng.mil/About/default.aspx.

3 *Schenck v. United States*, 249 U.S. 47 (1919).

4 Jennifer De Pinto, "2nd Amendment Supreme Court Case: Poll Shows Public Split on Gun Rights," CBS News, June 28, 2010. http://www.cbsnews.com/8301-503544_162-20009088-503544.html.

5 Brady Center to Prevent Gun Violence Web site. http://www.bradycenter.org/about/.

6 *McDonald v. Chicago*, 561 U.S. ___, 130 S.Ct. 3020 (2010), Justice Scalia concurring opinion, at 12.

7 Gary Fields, "Washington's New Gun Rules Shift Constitutional Debate," *Wall Street Journal*, May 17, 2010. http://online.wsj.com/article/SB10001424052748704093204575216680860962548.html.

8 *McDonald*, at 39–40.

9 J. Scott Harr and Karen M. Hess, *Constitutional Law and the Criminal Justice System* (Belmont, Calif.: Thomson Wadsworth, 2005), p. 164.

10 Michael A. Bellesiles, *Arming America: The Origins of a National Gun Culture* (Brooklyn, N.Y.: Soft Skull Press, 2000).

11 Zack Burgess, "Study: More Guns, More Killing," *Philadelphia Tribune*, October 18, 2009.

12 Eric H. Monkkonen, *Murder in New York City* (Berkeley: University of California Press, 2001).

13 Jon Wiener, "Fire at Will: How the Critics Shot Up Michael Bellesiles's Book *Arming America*," *Nation* (November 4, 2002), p. 28. http://www.thenation.com/article/fire-will?page=full. Emory University news release, October 25, 2002. http://www.emory.edu/central/NEWS/Releases/bellesiles1035563546.html.

Counterpoint: The Second Amendment Remains Relevant

1 John Adams, *A Defense of the Constitutions of Government in the United States of America*, 1787–1788.

2 Cesare Beccaria, *On Crimes and Punishments* (*Dei delitti e delle pene*, 1764). Translation by H. Paulucci, 1963 (New Brunswick, N.J.: Transaction Publishers, 2009).

3 *The Federalist Papers*, No. 46.

4 *The Federalist Papers*, No. 29.

5 *The Federalist Papers*, Nos. 184–188.

6 Akhil Reed Amar and Alan Hirsch, *For the People: What the Constitution Really Says about Your Rights* (New York: Free Press, 1998).

7 Albert Gallatin, letter to Alexander Addison, October 7, 1789. From Stephen Halbrook, *That Every Man Be Armed: The Evolution of a Constitutional Right* (Albuquerque: University of New Mexico Press, 1984), p. 225.

8 *United States v. Verdugo-Urquidez*, 494 U.S. 259 (1990).

9 *District of Columbia v. Heller*, 128 S.Ct. 2783 (2008).

10 *McDonald v. Chicago*, 561 U.S. ___, 130 S.Ct. 3020 (2010).

11 Charlton Heston, "Winning the Culture War," American Rhetoric Online Speech Bank, delivered February 16, 1999, Austin Hall, Harvard Law School. http://www.americanrhetoric.com/speeches/charltonhestonculturalwar.htm.

12 William J. Vizzard, *Shots in the Dark: The Policy, Politics, and Symbolism of Gun Control* (Lanham, Md.: Rowman & Littlefield, 2000), p. 113.

Point: Gun-Control Laws Reduce Violence

1 Bill Marsh, "An Accounting of Daily Gun Deaths," *New York Times*, April 21, 2007. http://www.nytimes.com/imagepages/2007/04/21/weekinreview/20070422_MARSH_GRAPHIC.html.

2 Violence Policy Center Web site, "Gun Violence in America." http://www.vpc.org/nrainfo/phil.html.

3 Franklin Zimring and Gordon Hawkins, *Crime Is Not the Problem: Lethal Violence in America* (New York: Oxford University Press, 1997).

4 *WISQARS Leading Causes of Death Reports, 1999–2007*, National Center for Injury Prevention and Control, Centers for Disease Control and Prevention. http://webappa.cdc.gov/sasweb/ncipc/leadcaus10.html.

5 Federal Bureau of Investigation, *Crime in the United States—1991 and 1997*.

6 Federal Bureau of Investigation Web site, *Crime in the United States, 2001*. http://www.fbi.gov/news/pressrel/press-releases/crime-in-the-united-states-2001-1.

7 Federal Bureau of Investigation Web site, *Crime in the United States—2008: Violent Crime*. http://www.fbi.gov/about-us/cjis/ucr/crime-in-the-u.s/2008.

8 John R. Lott Jr., *More Guns, Less Crime: Understanding Crime and Gun Control Laws* (Chicago: University of Chicago Press, 1998).

9 Violence Prevention Center Web site, "Funder of the Lott CCW Study Has Links to the Gun Industry." http://www.vpc.org/fact_sht/lottlink.htm. John R. Lott Jr., "Trigger Happy: Are the Major Media Frivolous or Biased?" *National Review* (June 22, 1998).

10 Brady Center to Prevent Gun Violence, *Concealed Truth: Concealed Weapons Laws and Trends in Violent Crime in the United States*, October 22, 1999.

11 Brady Campaign to Prevent Gun Violence Web site, "Gun Violence: Guns in America." http://www.bradycampaign.org/facts/gunsinamerica.

12 All material in this paragraph is from John Henry Sloan, Arthur L. Kellermann, et al., "Handgun Regulations, Crime, Assaults, and Homicide: A Tale of Two Cities," *New England Journal of Medicine* 319, No. 19 (November 10, 1988), p. 1256.

13 *The Brady Handgun Violence Prevention Act*, Public Law 103-159, 103d Cong., 1st sess. (November 30, 1993).

14 Brady Campaign to Prevent Gun Violence Web site, "Federal Gun Laws: Brady Background Checks." http://www.bradycampaign.org/legislation/backgroundchecks/.

15 Ibid.

16 President Bill Clinton, speech at the Ohio Peace Officers Training Academy, February 15, 1994.

17 Marianne W. Zawitz, "Guns Used in Crime," Bureau of Justice Statistics, July 1995, NCJ-14820.

18 Brady Campaign to Prevent Gun Violence Web site, "Federal Gun Laws: Assault-Style Weapons." http://www.

bradycampaign.org/legislation/
msassaultweapons.

19 U.S. Departments of Justice and Treasury, *Gun Shows: Brady Checks and Crime Gun Traces*, January 1999.

20 Library of Congress, "Bill Summary and Status," Thomas Legislative Services. http://www.thomas.gov/cgi-bin/bdquery/z?d111:SN00843.

21 Bureau of Justice Statistics Web site, "Homicide Trends in the U.S." http://bjs.ojp.usdoj.gov/content/homicide/gender.cfm.

22 Josh Sugarmann, *Every Handgun Is Aimed at You: The Case for Banning Handguns* (New York: New Press, 2001).

23 Matthew Miller and David Hemenway, "Guns and Suicide in the United States," *New England Journal of Medicine* 359, No. 10 (September 4, 2008), p. 989.

24 Associated Press, "Guns as Likely to Kill Kids in Rural Areas," MSNBC.com, May 24, 2010. http://www.msnbc.msn.com/id/37305279/ns/health-kids_and_parenting/.

Counterpoint: Gun Control Does Not Prevent Crime

1 William J. Vizzard, *Shots in the Dark* (Lanham, Md.: Rowman & Littlefield, 2000).

2 Bureau of Justice Statistics, *Historical Statistics on Prisoners in State and Federal Institutions, Year End 1925–1986.* Bureau of Justice Statistics, *Correctional Populations in the United States, 1987–1994.*

3 Death Penalty Information Center Web site, "Murder Rates Nationally and by State." http://www.deathpenaltyinfo.org/murder-rates-nationally-and-state.

4 National Rifle Association Institute for Legislative Action Web site, "The Case for Reforming the District of Columbia's Gun Laws," March 28, 2007. http://www.nraila.org/Issues/FactSheets/Read.aspx?id=72. National Rifle Association Institute for Legislative Action Web site, "The War Against Handguns," February 15, 2001. http://www.nraila.org/issues/factsheets/read.aspx?id=17. National Rifle Association Institute for Legislative Action Web site, "Ballistic

Fingerprinting—The Maryland Example: Costing Taxpayers Without Benefiting Law Enforcement," October 21, 2002. http://www.nraila.org/Issues/FactSheets/Read.aspx?id=97&issue=078. Sandra S. Froman, "California Gun Vilification: A Blueprint for America," National Rifle Association Institute for Legislative Action Web site, July 3, 2001. http://www.nraila.org/Issues/Articles/Read.aspx?ID=56.

5 Jens Ludwig and Philip J. Cook, "Homicide and Suicide Rates Associated with Implementation of the Brady Handgun Violence Prevention Act," *Journal of the American Medical Association* 284, No. 5 (August 2, 2000), p. 585.

6 Don B. Kates, "Gun Laws Around the World: Do They Work?" *American Guardian* (October 1997), pp. 48–49, 60–62.

7 Gary Kleck and Marc Gertz, "Armed Resistance to Crime: The Prevalence and Nature of Self-Defense with a Gun," *Journal of Criminal Law and Criminology* 86 (Fall 1995), p. 164.

8 John R. Lott Jr., *More Guns, Less Crime: Understanding Crime and Gun Control Laws* (Chicago: University of Chicago Press, 1998).

9 Gary Kleck, "Crime Control Through the Private Use of Armed Force," *Social Problems* 35, No. 1 (February 1988), p. 15.

10 David B. Kopel, "Lawyers, Guns, and Burglars," *Arizona Law Review* 43 (Summer 2001), p. 345.

11 Matthew Bigg, "Southern U.S. Town Proud of Its Mandatory Gun Law," Reuters.com, April 18, 2007. http://www.reuters.com/article/idUSN1719257620070418.

12 U.S. Department of Justice, Law Enforcement Assistance Administration, *Rape Victimization in 26 American Cities* (Washington, D.C.: U.S. Government Printing Office, 1979), p. 31.

13 John R. Lott Jr., *More Guns, Less Crime: Understanding Crime and Gun Control Laws*, 3rd ed. (Chicago: University of Chicago Press, 2010), pp. 264–265.

14 Ibid., p. 164.

15 Ibid., p. 20.

16 U.S. Department of Justice, National Institute of Justice, *The Armed Criminal in America; A Survey of Incarcerated Felons* (Washington, D.C.: U.S. Government Printing Office, July 1985).

17 Gary Kleck, *Targeting Guns: Firearms and Their Control* (Hawthorne, N.Y.: Aldine de Gruyter, 1997).

Point: Manufacturers Should Share in Guns' Costs to Society

1 U.S. Centers for Disease Control and Prevention, *National Vital Statistics Reports* 49, No. 8 (September 21, 2001), p. 10. http://www.cdc.gov/nchs/data/nvsr/nvsr49/nvsr49_08.pdf. U.S. Centers for Disease Control and Prevention, *National Vital Statistics Reports* 50, No. 15 (September 16, 2002), p. 10. http://www.cdc.gov/nchs/data/nvsr/nvsr50/nvsr50_15.pdf.

2 Associated Press, "Surprising Fact: Half of Gun Deaths Are Suicides," MSNBC.com, June 30, 2008. http://www.msnbc.msn.com/id/25463844/.

3 Allan Lengel, "The Price of Urban Violence," *Washington Post*, December 28, 1997.

4 Philip J. Cook and Jens Ludwig, *Gun Violence: The Real Costs* (Oxford: Oxford University Press, 2000), pp. 10–11. Kenneth W. Kizer, Mary J. Vassar, et al., "Hospitalization Charges, Costs, and Income for Firearm-Related Injuries at a University Trauma Center," *Journal of the American Medical Association* 273, No. 22 (June 14, 1995), p. 1,768. Wendy Max and Dorothy P. Rice, "Shooting in the Dark: Estimating the Cost of Firearm Injuries," *Health Affairs* 12, No. 4 (Winter 1993), p. 171.

5 *Protection of Lawful Commerce in Arms Act of 2005*, Public Law 109-92, 109th Cong., 1st sess. (October 25, 2005).

6 Violence Policy Center news release, "New VPC Report Details How Liability Legislation (H.R. 2366) Would Protect Manufacturers of Guns Used in 1999 Columbine Massacre," February 15, 2000. http://www.vpc.org/press/0002dead.htm.

7 Dina El Boghdady, "New Wal-Mart Policy Stiffens Requirements for Gun Sales," *Washington Post*, July 4, 2002.

8 Andy Grimm, "Lawsuit Against Gunmakers, Dealers Still in Play," *Post-Tribune of Northwest Indiana*, June 30, 2010.

Counterpoint: Gun Manufacturers Are Not Responsible for Gun-Related Deaths

1 John Lott, "Gun Shy: Cities Turn from Regulation to Litigation in Their Campaign Against Guns," *National Review* (December 21, 1998), p. 46.

2 Robert A. Levy, "None of Their Business," *National Review* (May 22, 2002). http://www.nationalreview.com/comment/comment-levy052202.asp.

3 *Protection of Lawful Commerce in Arms Act of 2005*, Public Law 109-92, 109th Cong., 1st sess. (October 25, 2005).

4 Jeff Reh, testifying in support of the *Protection of Lawful Commerce in Arms Act.*, on April 18, 2002, to the House Subcommittee on Commerce, Trade, and Consumer Protection.

5 Jenny Miao Jiang, "Regulating Litigation Under the Protection of Lawful Commerce in Arms Act: Economic Activity or Regulatory Nullity?" *Albany Law Review* 70, No. 2 (2007), pp. 537–538.

6 Ibid.

Conclusion: The Future of Gun Control in the United States

1 *McDonald v. Chicago*, 561 U.S. ___, 130 S.Ct. 3020 (2010), at 44.

2 Ibid., at 39–40.

3 Brady Campaign to Prevent Gun Violence Web site, "Gun Lobby-Backed Efforts: Federal Concealed Carry." http://www.bradycampaign.org/legislation/gunlobbybacked/fedccw.

4 Ibid.

5 Brady Campaign to Prevent Gun Violence Web site, "Gun Lobby-Backed Efforts: Open Carry Guns." http://www.bradycampaign.org/legislation/gunlobbybacked/opencarryguns.

6 Eric Kelderman, "Campus Gun Bans Are Still on Solid Ground, Legal Experts Say," *Chronicle of Higher Education*

Web site, June 29, 2010. http://
chronicle.com/article/Campus-Gun-
Bans-Are-Still-on/66089/?sid=at&utm_
source=at&utm_medium=en.

7 Scott Mayerowitz, "Visitors to National
Parks Can Now Carry Guns," ABCNews.
com, February 22, 2010. http://abcnews.
go.com/Travel/guns-national-parks-fire-
arms-now-allowed-yellowstone-yosem-
ite/story?id=9910171&page=3.

8 Greg Bluestein, "Starbucks Gun Policy:
Refusal to Ban Firearms Pleases Open
Carry Advocates, Troubles Gun Control
Advocates," *Huffington Post*, February
28, 2010. http://www.huffingtonpost.
com/2010/02/28/starbucks-gun-policy-
refu_n_480062.html.

9 U.S. General Accounting Office, *Potential Effects of Next-Day Destruction of
NICS Background Check Records*, July

2002. http://www.gao.gov/new.items/
d02653.pdf.

10 Audrey Hudson, "Gun Program for
Pilots Set for Expansion, Officials
Insist," *Washington Times*, March, 24,
2009. http://www.washingtontimes.
com/news/2009/mar/24/gun-program-
for-pilots-set-for-expansion-officials/.

11 Sally B. Donnelly, "Are We Ready for
Pilots Packing Heat?" *Time*, September
2, 2002.

12 Hudson, "Gun Program for Pilots Set
for Expansion, Officials Insist."

13 Josh Sugarmann, *Every Handgun Is
Aimed at You: The Case for Banning
Handguns* (New York: New Press, 2001).

14 Anna Quindlen, *Thinking Out Loud: On
the Personal, the Political, the Public, and
the Private* (New York: Random House,
1993), p. 19.

Books and Articles

Amar, Akhil Reed. "The Bill of Rights and the Fourteenth Amendment." *Yale Law Journal* 101(1992): 1193.

Cook, Philip J. *Gun Violence: The Real Costs.* Oxford, U.K.: Oxford University Press, 2002.

Cook, Philip J., and Jens Ludwig. *Litigation as Regulation: The Case of Firearms.* Terry Sanford Institute of Public Policy, Duke University, Working Papers Series SAN01–09, March 2001.

Kellermann, Arthur L., Frederick P. Rivara, et al. "Gun Ownership as a Risk Factor for Homicide in the Home," *New England Journal of Medicine* 329, No. 15 (October 7, 1993).

Kleck, Gary. *Point Blank: Guns and Violence in America.* Hawthorne, N.Y.: Aldine de Gruyter, 1991.

———. *Targeting Guns: Firearms and Their Control.* Hawthorne, N.Y.: Aldine de Gruyter, 1997.

Kleck, Gary, and Marc Gertz. "Armed Resistance to Crime: The Prevalence and Nature of Self-Defense with a Gun," *Journal of Criminal Law and Criminology* 86, No. 1 (Autumn1995).

Kopel, David B. *The Samurai, the Mountie, and the Cowboy: Should America Adopt the Gun Controls of Other Democracies?* Buffalo, N.Y.: Prometheus, 1992.

Anti–Gun Control

Baldridge, Pjeter D. ed. *Gun Ownership and the Second Amendment.* Hauppage, N.Y.: Nova Science Publishers, 2009.

Charles, Patrick J. *The Second Amendment: The Intent and Its Interpretation by the States and the Supreme Court.* Jefferson, N.C.: McFarland, 2009.

Cottrol, Robert J., ed. *Gun Control and the Constitution: Sources and Explorations on the Second Amendment.* New York: Garland, 1994.

Doherty, Brian. *Gun Control on Trial: Inside the Supreme Court Battle Over the Second Amendment.* Washington, D.C.: Cato Institute, 2008.

Eggen, Dan. "Domestic Abusers Bought Guns." *Washington Post*, June 26, 2002.

Halbrook, Stephen P. *The Founders' Second Amendment: Origins of the Right to Bear Arms.* Chicago: Ivan R. Dee, 2008.

Halbrook, Stephen. *That Every Man Be Armed: The Evolution of a Constitutional Right.* Albuquerque: University of New Mexico Press, 1984.

Henderson, Harry. *Library in a Book: Gun Control.* New York: Facts On File, 2000.

Kates, Don B. "Handgun Prohibition and the Original Meaning of the Second Amendment." *Michigan Law Review* 82 (1983).

Kellermann, Arthur L., Frederick P. Rivara, et al. "Suicide in the Home in Relation to Gun Ownership." *New England Journal of Medicine* 327, No. 7 (August 13, 1992).

Kleck, Gary, and Don B. Kates. *Armed: New Perspectives on Gun Control.* Amherst, N.Y.: Prometheus Books, 2001.

Kopel, David B, ed. *Guns: Who Should Have Them?* Amherst, N.Y.: Prometheus, 1995.

Levinson, Sanford. "The Embarrassing Second Amendment." *Yale Law Journal* 99, No. 3 (December 1989).

Levy, Robert A. "None of Their Business," *National Review*, May 22, 2002. Available online. URL: http://www.nationalreview.com/comment/comment-levy052202.asp

Lott, John R. Jr. *More Guns, Less Crime: Understanding Crime and Gun Control Laws.* Chicago: University of Chicago Press, 1998.

Malcolm, Joyce Lee. *To Keep and Bear Arms: The Origins of an Anglo-American Right.* Cambridge, Mass.: Harvard University Press, 1994.

Poe, Richard. *The Seven Myths of Gun Control: Reclaiming the Truth about Guns, Crime, and the Second Amendment.* Westminster, Md.: Prima, 2001.

Pro–Gun Control

Quindlen, Anna. *Thinking Out Loud: On the Personal, the Political, the Public, and the Private.* New York: Random House, 1993.

Sloan, John Henry, Arthur L. Kellermann, et al. "Handgun Regulations, Crime, Assaults, and Homicide: A Tale of Two Cities." *New England Journal of Medicine* 319, No. 19 (November 10, 1988).

Spitzer, Robert J. *Gun Control: A Documentary and Reference Guide.* Westport, Conn.: Greenwood Press, 2009.

———. *The Politics of Gun Control.* Washington, D.C.: CQ Press, 2004.

Sugarmann, Josh. *Every Handgun Is Aimed at You: The Case for Banning Handguns.* New York: New Press, 2001.

U.S. Government Accounting Office. *Potential Effects of Next-Day Destruction of NICS Background Check Records,* July 2002. Available online. URL: http://www.gao.gov/new.items/d02653.pdf

Uviller, Richard H., and William G. Merkel. *The Militia and the Right to Arms: Or, How the Second Amendment Fell Silent.* Durham, N.C.: Duke University Press, 2002.

Van Alstyne, William. "The Second Amendment and the Personal Right to Arms." *Duke Law Journal* 43, No. 6 (April 1994).

Vizzard, William J. *Shots in the Dark.* Lanham, Md.: Rowman & Littlefield, 2000.

Volokh, Eugene. "The Commonplace Second Amendment." *New York University Law Review* 73, No. 3 (June 1998).

Zawitz, Marianne W. *Guns Used in Crime.* U.S. Bureau of Justice Statistics, July 1995, NCJ-14820.

Web Sites

American Bar Association Standing Committee on Gun Violence
http://www.abanet.org/gunviol/
> This section of the American Bar Association's Web site presents a moderate pro-gun-control position. The links page connects to archives of court decisions, material on gun laws and regulations, organizations with varying positions, and descriptions of gun-control policies outside the United States.

The Brady Campaign to Prevent Gun Violence
http://www.bradycampaign.org
> One of the strongest voices in the debate about gun control. Advocates strongly for gun control but also provides some neutral information, such as congressional voting records, summaries of current and pending legislation, and material on laws by state. See also the campaign's sister organization, the Brady Center to Prevent Gun Violence, http://www.bradycenter.org.

The Brady Center's Legal Action Project
http://www.gunlawsuits.org
> The litigation arm of the Brady Center to Prevent Gun Violence. Provides litigation updates and legal arguments in favor of gun control.

Bureau of Alcohol, Tobacco, Firearms, and Explosives
http://www.atf.gov/
> Includes reports on crime trends, as well as a great deal of other information essential to the debate.

Federal Bureau of Investigation Uniform Crime Reports
http://www.fbi.gov/ucr/ucr.htm
> Among the most thorough and most reliable sources of statistics on crimes of all kinds.

The Journalist's Guide to Gun Policy Scholars and Second Amendment Scholars
http://www.gunscholar.org
> This list of scholars who are "skeptical of gun control," compiled by Professor Eugene Volokh of UCLA Law School, includes not only specialties and contact information, but also useful lists of publications and some links to matter such as congressional testimony. A separate page on the site gives a politically broader selection of links to organizations and information on the topic, although it is more or less weighted against gun control.

National Center for Policy Analysis
http://www.ncpa.org
> A multi-issue conservative think tank that takes detailed pro-gun positions.

National Rifle Association
http://www.nra.org
> Perhaps the center of the anti-gun-control side of the debate. Offers many pro-gun arguments, position papers, legislative updates, links to articles, and much more.

U.S. Department of JusticeBureau of Justice Statistics
http://bjs.ojp.usdoj.gov/
> Offers figures on crime victimization.

U.S. Sentencing Commission
http://www.ussc.gov
> Includes detailed figures on federal crimes and sentencing.

Violence Policy Center
http://www.vpc.org

A major proponent of gun control, possibly more intensely opposed to firearms in general than is the Brady Center/Brady Campaign.

PICTURE CREDITS ///// ▷

PAGE

13: Dennis Brack BSB 7/Newscom
43: Carr/MCT/Newscom
48: s70/ZumaPress/Newscom

62: Yingling/MCT/Newscom
83: k94/Zuma Press/Newscom

ANGELA VALDEZ lives in Philadelphia, Pennsylvania. A graduate of New York University, she has reported for several newspapers, including *Newsday*, the *Flint Journal*, and the *Philadelphia Inquirer*.

JOHN E. FERGUSON JR. is a lecturer at the Hankamer School of Business and in the political science department at Baylor University in Waco, Texas. He earned his M.T.S. and J.D. degrees from Vanderbilt University's Divinity and Law Schools. He has been a member of the bar in Tennessee, Washington, D.C., and the United States Supreme Court.

ALAN MARZILLI, M.A., J.D., lives in Washington, D.C., and is a senior writer for Advocates for Human Potential, Inc., a research and consulting firm based in Sudbury, Mass., and Albany, N.Y. He primarily works on developing training and educational materials for agencies of the federal government on topics such as housing, mental health policy, employment, and transportation. He has spoken on mental health issues in 30 states, the District of Columbia, and Puerto Rico; his work has included training mental health administrators, nonprofit management and staff, and people with mental illnesses and their families on a wide variety of topics, including effective advocacy, community-based mental health services, and housing. He has written several handbooks and training curricula that are used nationally and as far away as the territory of Guam. He managed statewide and national mental health advocacy programs and worked for several public interest lobbying organizations while studying law at Georgetown University. He has written more than a dozen books, including numerous titles in the POINT/COUNTERPOINT series.